To

from Bill

ALSO BY WILLIAM HUMPHREY

The Last Husband and Other Stories

Home from the Hill

The Ordways

A Time and a Place

The Spawning Run

Proud Flesh

*Ah, Wilderness! The Frontier
in American Literature*

FARTHER OFF FROM HEAVEN

WILLIAM
HUMPHREY

FARTHER OFF
FROM HEAVEN

Alfred A. Knopf   New York   1977

Library of Congress Cataloging in Publication Data
Humphrey, William.   Farther off from heaven.
    1. Humphrey, William—Biography—Youth.
2. Authors, American—20th century—Biography.
                    I. Title.
  PS3558.U464Z52   813'.5'4 [B]   76-47936
            ISBN 0-394-41188-9

TO MY MOTHER

I REMEMBER, I REMEMBER

THE FIR TREES DARK AND HIGH;

I USED TO THINK THEIR SLENDER TOPS

WERE CLOSE AGAINST THE SKY:

IT WAS A CHILDISH IGNORANCE.

BUT NOW 'TIS LITTLE JOY

TO KNOW I'M FARTHER OFF FROM HEAVEN

THAN WHEN I WAS A BOY.

—*Thomas Hood*

The names of some of the people

who figure in this account

have been changed to spare them

or their survivors

pain or embarrassment.

I

"SON! WAKE UP! Wake up! Son, wake up!"

My mother's voice came to me as though through water. I could sense her urgency, but trying to wake was like trying to save myself from drowning—or rather, like having given up trying to save myself, surrendering to it. Consciousness shone dimly above me, like sunlight from under water, but after each effort to rise to it, my tired mind sank back deeper into the soothing dark.

"Son! Wake up! Wake up! Son, wake up!"

I felt myself being shaken, as one is when he is brought out of the water dying. I could no more wake up than I could come back to life.

I had been permitted to stay up late the evening before, and the evening before that, to celebrate the Fourth of July, and I was just turned thirteen. I had never before been wakened at three o'clock in the morning.

THE FOURTH OF JULY fell that year—1937—on a Sunday. This, in a county town like ours, Clarksville, Texas, meant that there was no Sunday that week but rather two Saturdays.

Saturday in Clarksville was always a holiday, the day when everybody came to town—Sundays when nobody did. Children were free from school, and from Sunday's sanctimonies and restraints. The stores, with all their wares, their wonders, were open; and even when you could not buy, you too could look. Food forbidden to you all week you were allowed to buy from the street vendors who appeared that day. Stand for just an hour anywhere on the public square, and the tireless circling of shoppers and strollers brought round to you in turn all your kinfolks and most everybody you knew from all over Red River County. Miss somebody and it was cause to wonder whether something was wrong with him. The square, being nobody's dwelling place, was everybody's gathering place. Not even above the shops, on the second and third floors, did anybody live; up there were offices and storerooms. Not used much during the week, the square on Saturday became the town's reception room, its public parlor.

And on Sunday, strewn with paper cups, bags, popcorn boxes, hot tamale shucks, fruit peels, peanut hulls, the shops dark and the shades drawn, it was like a parlor the morning after a late-night party.

But that year, throughout the entire weekend just past, downtown Clarksville had been so clogged with cars and people that motorists passing through headed west toward Paris or east toward Texarkana on U.S. 82, which ran through the square, had been detoured around our festivities through residential streets.

On Saturday morning there had been a parade, with the high-school band and the local Boy Scout troop in their uniforms, veterans of three wars in theirs: bobbing along in the lead, our two surviving Confederate grays, like the last living pair of passenger pigeons, U.S. Army khakis from the Spanish-American and what was then called The World War, followed by merchants' and tradesmen's floats, on one of which I had ridden, my costume a suit of striped coveralls, a miniature of those my father wore to work, with the emblem of his and his partner's auto repair and body shop sewn on the back. I was so proud of those coveralls that for the rest of the weekend I could not be gotten out of them short of skinning me.

By noon that day no parade could have made its way downtown. Cars in the street moved as one, when they moved at all, like the linked coaches of a train. The square was getting to look, even on ordinary Saturdays, like the end of a Detroit assembly line. More and more cars appeared there weekly, and round and around they drove all day and into the night, the riders goggling out and being goggled at like goldfish in a bowl. Today every child out of infancy had been down on the square since breakfast—no fear of one's getting lost: everybody knew whose you were; now, their housework done, their mothers joined them. The tradesmen who could—unlike my father, whose busiest weekend of the year this was— shut up shop and came to swell the throng.

Meanwhile, from out in the country, farmfolks streamed in in greater numbers than had ever been seen there before, as though there had been an increase in their population. Increasingly motorized was what they were, and better able to get there, and, in 1937, they had something to celebrate. Nobody was saying any more that prosperity was just around the corner; but at least our regional troubles no longer compounded the depression for us: the long drought had been broken, the dust storms had blown themselves out, and just now, at just the right time for it, the prairies surrounding Clarksville were whitening a little more each morning with the cotton on which we all depended as though in the night fresh snow had fallen—snow in July being no more improbable to us, on whom it never fell, than snow at any other time of year. Things were looking up—one sign of it: during those two days I had been given no less than seventy cents by men on the square, not one of them under obligation of kinship to me, just friends and acquaintances who, moved by the holiday mood and the generally brightened outlook, and mindful of my reputation as a good boy, had stopped me in my play to ask, "Billy, how would you like to have a nickel?" With that money I had offered to pay a little on my large, long overdue bill at Athas's Confectionery, but my friend Jim, the owner and head kitchen magician, insisted on extending my credit.

There had been platform speaking on the shaded lawn of the courthouse, three blocks north of the square —one of that year's guest speakers the young Lyndon Johnson. On Saturday afternoon out at the Old Fair Grounds north of town, a baseball game; on Sunday, after sparsely attended church services (my own scheduled confirmation had been patriotically postponed), a barbecue and another baseball game out at the New Fair Grounds west of town, followed after dark by a fireworks display.

The summer days were long, and for the past two, time went uncounted, the chimes of the courthouse clock muffled by the daylong drone of motors, the cackling of horns, the burst of firecrackers, the blare and thump of jukeboxes in the cafes and the drugstores and the shouts of children playing around the Confederate monument in the center of the plaza and chasing one another among the parked cars.

That was my town square only somewhat livelier than I was used to seeing it, and as I had last seen it just hours earlier. Now at three o'clock on Monday morning, minutes after my mother had wakened me with a look of fear such as I had seen on her face just once before, the square bore to that familiar and vivid image the relation of a photographic negative to the print—

ashes to a fire—a darkened stageset after the play is over and the actors and the audience have left the theater. That other time, my mother had been afraid for my life. I thought that she was afraid for me now, and this made me afraid for myself. What was wrong with me?

"Get dressed as quick as you can!" my mother said. "Your daddy has been hurt."

One light shone from a second story window on the southeast corner of the square, and at the curb there sat parked the only car. That lone light, except for the corner streetlamps, was the only light we had seen burning on our drive downtown. We and whoever occupied that office were the only people awake. In that stillness, our car as we drove toward the light made a sound as loud, it seemed to me, as all the cars of Saturday.

Our presence there at that hour brought someone to investigate. We had parked beside the other car and gotten onto the sidewalk when, from around the corner, lancing the darkness, came the beam of a flashlight, footsteps, a man: the town nightwatchman. This local figure had always been a bit of a goblin to me. I thought of him as something like the town watchdog and imagined him as fierce and unappeasable, with a particular animosity toward boys. I had occasionally glimpsed him emerging at dark from wherever he spent the day, carrying, on a strap around his neck, the big nightclock which kept the curfew hours taken from us children and which we were given back just when we did not want them, when we were too sick or too unhappy to sleep. I thought of him whenever I opened one of the little lidded metal containers—and I never passed one without opening it —that were affixed to the walls of the buildings at the four corners of the square, and taking from it the chained key to his clock, each different in cut, by the use of which he established that he had faithfully made his nightly rounds. Actually to encounter him now in his element was as eerie as sighting a nightowl. For him it was even more startling than for us, for it was not unnatural that he be there, it was his territory, his accustomed hour. We skirted one another in passing like different species, the one nocturnal, the other abroad on some untoward errand.

Upstairs my mother and I entered the doctor's office, unfamiliar to me because he was not our doctor. I thought I caught a quick look on his face of suggestion, of warning, meant, though aimed over my head, for me. If so, it only made my mother grip my hand still tighter, and we were shown together into the room that gave onto the square.

What I saw stretched on the tabletop looked like a scarecrow thrown there. Its clothes, a suit of coveralls exactly like my own, were dyed with blood, stained with motor oil, ripped and slashed, and the entire body so swollen it seemed to have been stuffed into them. The legs and arms were splayed, twisted, limp. The chest on one side was crushed, forcing out the other side. It looked as if it had been hanged, trampled, like the defiled effigy of a man.

I had many times seen my father's face black with the grease of his trade; now it was bruised black, caked with blood, and so battered and lacerated that it was necessary for me to piece it back together from memory —so thoroughly disfigured that although it was just hours since I had last seen him, it was hard to recollect and reassemble his features. The right eye was gone.

Above the empty socket was a deep depression in the forehead, above the other eye—puffed shut—a large bulge. The nose was cleft. The jaw hung open and wrenched awry, the lips were drawn back baring the gums, the gaps among the teeth—always so regular and so white—and the shattered ones, brown with blood, that remained.

His breathing had a sound known to me. It was the sound of a drowning person drawing his last breath. Only this was one drowning from inside, on his own blood.

I longed to be in my bed, where I was supposed to be—to sink back into that deep sleep I had been shaken out of. Or had I? Surely I must be asleep and having a bad dream. Only in dreams could so short a time bring so great a change in things. Everybody else was asleep; so should I be. Back in bed I would go over my plans for tomorrow and, hugging them to me, would drift off. Morning would come as it always had. Things would be as they had always been.

I heard the strange doctor telling my mother that the ambulance was on its way.

Things would never be the same for me again. Through the window above my father's broken, bloody body, in the darkness shrouding the town square, I could make out nothing. I felt slip from me in that moment not only the certainty of my future but the fixity of my past. It was as if I had been wakened out of my childhood.

IT WAS IN A CAR ACCIDENT—if it could be called that—that my father had been hurt. The words I had heard

my mother say to him many times came back to me now
(I wondered if she was recalling them, too): "Clarence,
you're going to kill yourself one of these days, and the
way you drive, it won't be an accident." I worried instead
that somebody else was going to kill him, and I had
for two years, ever since he began carrying the pistol.

It was not a target pistol, not a sporting arm; I knew
that, and I knew guns. Nor was carrying it concealed
on him the way a sporting arm was carried. It was not,
as .22's were promoted in the ads in the outdoors magazines, for "plinking." That pistol of his was a man-killer.

My father never explained what threat or what fear
made him carry the pistol, a .280 Colt automatic in a
quick-draw holster nestled in his left armpit, and so I
did not know why—or rather, I did know, precisely because he did not explain it, and because I knew why the
men in the movies carried them, as men in so many of
the movies of that era did, especially the one who, in looks,
build, bearing, attitudes, personality, even in his expres-
sions, was so much like my father that watching him on
the screen frightened me far beyond the intended scari-
ness of his role, perhaps because, even so, I still found him
appealing: I mean James Cagney—not the song-and-
dance-man Cagney, but Cagney the gangster-film star.
To me there was nothing unreal or even remote in those
bloody gun battles, those ambushes and shoot-outs and
careening car chases; to me they were everyday. In the
talk on the streetcorners and in the barber shop and in
my father's garage, in the newspapers I delivered each
afternoon, the main topic was the exploits of desperadoes
still on the loose and others only recently eradicated:
Dillinger, Ma Barker's boys, Pretty Boy Floyd, Machine-
gun Kelly, Clyde Barrow and Bonnie Parker, as well as

one local would-be badman, my own father's younger brother, caught not long ago in the attempted burglary of a cafe across the square from where we now sat waiting for the ambulance to arrive, and serving a sentence in the State penitentiary in Huntsville. My father had the pistol on him now—I had seen the bulge. That second button from the top of his coveralls: it had not been torn open in the collision; it was always left unbuttoned for instant access to the pistol: his equalizer. For he was a little man in a place where men grew tall, sensitive about his size and thus ready, as my mother said of him admiringly, "to fight a circular saw," touchy, not to be trifled with, a pilot-light burning in him always, quick to flare into flame at any slight, any dare, any slur, mean when riled and a dirty fighter, as little men must be: a sawed-off shotgun of a man, that was what my father was—or had been.

A SINGLE SWITCH seemed to have turned on the lights all along the street running west from the square as Clarksville was wakened by the wail of the siren like a household wakened by the cries of a child in the night. Wail followed wail breathlessly, rising in volume, mounting to shrieks.

So deep and so extensive was the silence of the night that the ambulance must still have been well beyond the outskirts when we first heard it; it swept downtown with the speed of a winter wind gusting in off the prairie. Through the window that looked westward and up the Paris road, I was watching for it, and saw the lights come on as though strung all on one wire. Our wait, measured by the spreading bloodstain on the sheet my father lay on, had been long; for Clarksville, county seat though it was, had no hospital, and Paris, site of the nearest one, was thirty-five miles away. Through it, my mother, who always cried easily, had not cried at all: proof to me, if proof had been needed, of the seriousness of my father's injuries. Only from time to time a whimper that she could not suppress escaped her, a catch in her breath became a sob.

In the empty bowl of the square the cry of the siren lingered on as though it was still going. We waited on the street for my father to be brought downstairs in the litter, and my mother squeezed my hand until it hurt. I endured it because I was afraid to draw her attention to it. She had always been a very protective mother, but now a new perception came to me through that link of our hands, one that took me at a leap into a new and unprepared phase of my life: my mother was clinging to me for support now, when never before had I felt so lost, so helpless.

My mind fumbled, trying to put back together the two pieces into which my life had just broken. Unequal pieces they were, and the terrifying part was that the one which ought to have been the big piece—my whole life up to just half an hour ago—was the little piece, and that half-hour was the big one. A gap of incongruousness separated the parts and kept them from reuniting: being up at this unnatural hour, driving through the familiar, suddenly unfamiliar streets, seeing the town square in this unknown aspect, seeing my father's unrecognizable body, hearing the peace of the night shattered by the sound of the siren—and the reminders of what had been only widened the break with them: the litter lying on the streets left over from the weekend celebrations, myself in the coveralls I had worn throughout them so proudly and unsuspectingly; these made them seem both more recent and more remote, realer and more unreal.

My father was brought down by the men in white and laid on the stretcher that stood waiting at the rear door of the ambulance. Sides were raised around the stretcher like those around a crib, then it was wheeled up the ramp, rolled inside, fastened to the floor. When the attendants emerged, my mother let go my aching hand and climbed inside. I followed her. We sat down on a bench that ran along the side. The door was closed on us.

The ambulance backed away from the curb and as we left the square the siren started up. People in their nightclothes, people whom I knew but who did not know that it was I inside, stood on their lighted porches to watch our passage. Though never before at night, I had heard and seen the ambulance from Paris come howling into town before, and had chased it, myself uninvolved in whatever calamity had brought it, morbidly curious along with the crowd. Now the calamity was mine, and I was the object of the morbid curiosity.

We had reached the outskirts of town when my father spoke. In a voice thickened to a gurgle, he said, "Turn out the lights." The lights were out, but all the way to Paris he groaned continuously, "Turn out the lights"—beyond reach of my mother's "Hush, darling, hush. We're with you, hear?"

While we went shrieking into the night that encircled the town like a frontier, my townspeople would be turning back indoors and switching off their lights and going back to bed, wondering what had happened and whom the ambulance had come for and saying to one another that they would learn all about it in the morning. I feared I might never see these people again. Wakened in the night, given no time to gather up my belongings or say goodbye to my lifelong friends, and hustled off into exile, I sought as I listened to my father's groans and the agonized wail of the siren above my head to impress upon my mind a map of my homeplace, to gather as many images and memories of it as I could before they faded: the square, the courthouse, the bridges over the creek, even the painful places—for the scars that life leaves on you are you, too: the vacant lot where you got hurt so badly, the bedroom where you spent the long and tedious recuperation, the wounds to the spirit—all, you must gather them all to you as you go into the unknown.

Superfluous effort! No wandering Jew ever carried with him a heavier freight of memories nor more of a sense of identification with a homeplace than I at thirteen, though unconfirmed in my faith, had already accumulated. By the waters of Babylon I would many times sit down and weep as I remembered my Zion, where all was familiar and friendly, where the seasons' difference was slight and slow, where the nights were patrolled by the watchman and kept quiet, where the clock in the courthouse tower chimed—as it had yesterday, as it would tomorrow—an hourly benediction upon the town, like an angelus, like a muezzin in his minaret calling the people to prayer.

II

To THIS DAY, wherever I may be, I never hear a town clock strike the hour but what, momentarily, a reddishness tints everything I see, and I smell an aroma so exquisitely appetizing that it must surely be ambrosia, the food of the gods.

Perhaps the notes are falling from the belfry of the *Mairie: un, deux, trois*, like the leaves from the tall plane trees. Perhaps from a campanile they plash into the time-worn bowl of the piazza like the drops of the fountain in its center: *uno, due, tre*. Perhaps they drift down like snowflakes from the steeple of some New England town meeting house. Not even a scene as remote from my early memories as St. Mark's in all its broken-down Byzantine splendor, or the Houses of Parliament and Westminster Abbey with Big Ben booming overhead, seen now through my eyes, is immune from this momentary reddening. The stink of the canals of Venice is sweetened for a moment by that smell. The statue in the town square of a *bersagliere* or a *poilu* turns into a Confederate foot-soldier with his bedroll on his back. The pigeons become martens and swallows. The belltower—be it Norman, Gothic, Romanesque, Baroque—becomes the tower of my courthouse, which was a marvelous muddle of all those styles. And though it lasts only for a moment, all is tinged that rosy red, suffused with that scent.

These visions and these sensations which the tolling of a town clock produces in me like an hallucinogenic drug date to the period when I learned to tell time by the chimes of the Clarksville courthouse clock. I could hear them from even the remotest part of town, and I could look up to read its face—or rather, one of its four faces, one of which was visible from almost any part of town, the courthouse being by far our tallest building. The coloration that time has for me comes from the clock's name. Why, I never knew, never asked, but apparently from the hour of 2:30 p.m. of May 27, 1885 —the first it ever struck—the clock was called "Old Red."

"What time is it?" was a question that people in Clarksville seldom asked one another. You did not have to have been listening for it to have heard Old Red's latest report. You were never out of sound of it. Yet it didn't seem in those unhurried times to be keeping watch over you. Rather, its deep, measured, authoritative yet fatherly tones seemed usually to be saying, "No rush. There's time." And even when it was later than you thought, the chimes were not a nagging but a gentle reminder. "There's Old Red telling me it's time for my dinner," people said. Or, "Old Red says it's time I was on my way."

Old Red's resonant notes regulated my steps to school, and that was at the hour when the town was waking to that appetizing smell. This came from the cottonseed mill at the northeast edge of town, beside the railroad tracks. The mill worked at night, as do bakeries, and so the town awoke to its fragrance as to that of fresh-baked bread, an aroma it resembled but was even more delicious than, and far more pervasive. Over the square in the early morning did hang the smell of fresh-baked bread, too, emanating from Ward's, the bakery on the north side—but the smell from the cottonseed mill hung over the entire town. Hard to believe that the golden yellow cottonseed meal was not edible, that it was fed to dairy cows.

A boy growing up in a small town gets to know it well, especially where the weather is mild the year round and keeps him much out of doors, and during a period, like mine, and in a place where change comes slowly. He starts school and goes through the grades with the same classmates. Occasionally one moves away or a new one comes to town, but not often. He is, or was in my time, taught by the same teachers who taught his parents. He is a part of a whole, like a coral-bank or a sponge: cells are added, cells die and fall away—the colony goes on, stays fixed.

I knew Clarksville very well, better than most of its adults did, for, as if making up for my inactive infancy, I came indoors only to roost. Quick to talk, slow to walk: I had been that kind of a child, so I was told. Indeed, if what I was told was true, I had been prodigiously quick at the one and downright retarded at the other. "Oh, look at the horse!" I was said to have said at the age of nine months. I had not walked until I was three years old. Now I was a rover and, in my mother's word, a "meddler," inquisitive to the degree of being a public nuisance—also perhaps making up for my early confinement—and I had lived in more different parts of the town than its oldest citizen, had walked across it to and from school by many different routes over my few but busy years.

We did not own a home. My parents, fresh from off the farm, were new to Clarksville. We could not afford to own a home, we rented; and we were continually moving. Houses for rent stood vacant in those depression years, and a vacant house could not be insured. Landlords waged a price war to attract tenants; as times worsened, they let them rent-free to families known to take good care of them. My mother had quickly earned herself a name around town as a good housekeeper—

"I believe in leaving a place cleaner than I found it,"
she said, ending, as she always did, "just like my mother
taught me"—and she had her pick of houses. Indeed,
she was in demand, wooed by landlords, who came
around often to make sure that everything was to her
liking, and who begged her to say what was wrong, why
she was leaving, whenever she announced that we were
moving, even when we were paying no rent. She would
leave a house because she had seen a mouse. My mother
was a restless one, never happier than on moving day—
such a chore for most women—even when we were
moving back now to a house we had lived in before, and
which, at the time, she could not get out of fast enough.
She sang and whistled as she packed the tubs and crates,
her hair wrapped in a rag. I was like her; I liked moving
often, too. I liked change. I liked exploring new neigh-
borhoods. In each I got to know better those of my
schoolmates who lived there; meanwhile, I was not
really saying goodbye to those I was leaving behind.
We must have lived in fifteen different houses scattered
around town in the course of some five years. One day
I came home from school and took a glass of milk and
a banana from the icebox, only to have a strange lady—
that is to say, a lady I knew, but who was not my mother
—come in and say, "Billy? Is that you? But you don't
live here any more, hon'. Did you forget? You all moved
out today and we moved in here. You live out on Third
Street now."

And so, when I remember Clarksville, it is not one
neighborhood, one block, one back yard, not one house
that I recall and see myself in (or if one house does stand
out from all the others, it is the one I would soonest forget, that one on Third Street, because in it I spent an

entire summer in bed, in it occurred the worst fight between my parents that I ever saw, and because it was the
one that burned down) but rather, because I lived in
so many different parts of it and spent so much of my
time out of doors, Clarksville itself is to me the house
I grew up in, my actual homes being the rooms of the
house, and the streets the hallways and the stairs, and
no less vivid, particular, intimate or full of associations
for me because of this diffuseness.

The grammar school—my grammar school—is gone
now. A later mayor of the town laid to rest forever the
thousands of small ghosts, mine among them, that
haunted those dark old halls, those classrooms where
the windows that both showed and shut out the world
beyond were a confinement worse than unlighted dun-
geons, ghosts with hearts too small for the unrequited
love that swelled them, the fear of failure and the terror
of tests on which one's parents' approval and love, the
teacher's favor, and the continued acceptance of one's
friends—in short, life itself—depended, by declaring the
building antiquated and unsafe and having it razed
and a new school erected on another site. But in my time
the grammar school stood where it always had, on a hill,
or what passed for a hill in our prairieland parts, on
the southwest edge of town. By the time I came along,
residential streets had spread beyond it out into the
countryside (Third Street was one of them), but not
very far, and it was not long since the schoolhouse had
stood where the town ended and farmfields began. It is
not unreasonable to suppose that the town had hoped to
insulate itself from the shouts, during recesses and the
lunch hour, of its noisiest element. To this placement,
and our continual moving, I owe my knowledge of my

home town. After I left it, thirty years and more were to pass before I saw it again, yet in all that time I carried in my mind a map of it that could, if printed, have guided a stranger to any address there he might be seeking. Perhaps it was the very violence with which I was torn from it—or it from me—that made my memory of it so indelible. They say that we would all like to escape from the rigors of life by getting back into the womb— I was from that womb untimely ripped. My childhood was amputated, and it ached as a missing limb continues to ache for the rest of your life.

THUS, SOMETIMES my way to school would take me across the bridge over the creek below the Presbyterian Church, then farther along, past the old open-sided tabernacle where, long ago, revival meetings had been held, but where now the pulpit tilted and the rickety pews were sinking to the ground as though the faith of whatever congregation it once sheltered had failed the test of doubt and time. Then on the street climbing to the school I would pass one of the many houses I had lived in—this the one where late one night I was hustled back to bed and out of the company of our unexpected guests, but not before learning that the lady, my own second-grade teacher, the only one on the faculty who was not an old maid as wrinkled as a raisin and as tough, but my own beautiful young Miss Lois, had on nothing underneath her borrowed raincoat, having lost her clothes, along with her sobriety, in a game of strip poker, and whose early retirement from a school system so strict that teachers were forbidden to marry, fired when they did, I may have hastened, much as I adored her, by telling this story in order to boast of Miss Lois's having visited my house, and in hopes that the meaning and the attraction, which I found so puzzling, of playing strip poker would be explained to me.

And, if that was my way to school, it would take me then past another house that I remembered—indeed, the one in which my memory began. Like drowning—and I say that not because of what came later, though what came later gives me the comparison—like coming to the surface (only to sink back again into the murk), I rose momentarily from darkness, long enough to remember light coming through a window in that house and curtains fluttering above my crib and looking down at me the face of the person whom until then I had known as a kitten or a puppy knows that creature it cries to, turns blindly to for milk, for warmth, and whom, now that my eyes were opened, I knew for my mother.

How long the time between that first memory of mine and the next one, I do not know; but if, instead of the route I have been retracing, my way to school was up College Avenue, as it was one year, then it would take me past the opening of the lane a short way down which stood the house—Mr. Jap Barry, the one-armed man's house—where it occurred. I was three then, and walking—for, excepting that moment in my crib, I remember nothing from the time, long as it was, when I could not walk—and exercising my newfound willfulness, too.

That morning I appeared at the breakfast table tousled and with grains of sleep in my eyes. When my mother reminded me to wash my face (she herself combed my hair—did so until I was twelve years old), I, for some reason, which is to say, for none, refused to do it. My mother was surprised, shocked, stunned, and instantly in dread of what she saw coming. She coaxed me, she pleaded with me. The more she pleaded the more stubbornly I refused. I know now that my mother was pleading with me to spare her this moment, which was bound to come sooner or later, and to spare myself the lifelong consequences of it, when she would have to discipline me, or rather, when she would have to reveal that she was incapable of disciplining the child, though she knew she should do so for his own good, who had cost her so much pain, whom she had pitied so deeply, and for whose imperfection at birth she blamed herself. My mother began to cry. This was the scene on which my father entered.

Himself freshly scrubbed, my father ordered me to go wash my face; when I refused, he too coaxed and pleaded with me. It was plain that my parents both lacked the courage to take the next step, and in my heart I gloated, thinking it was my will rather than their love for me that was prevailing, and not knowing what a harvest of future pain I was sowing for myself. At last, it was my father, obeying my mother's orders, who marched me in my nightshirt to the washstand on the back porch, where he himself poured the warm water from the kettle into the washpan for me, and ordered me to wash my face. I refused even to climb my stool. The order was repeated three times. My father then took off his belt and gave me three halfhearted licks with it. I felt no pain and I did not cry but I looked at him resentfully and that was enough. His eyes brimmed with tears. He left me and went back to the kitchen. I heard him tell my mother that he would never do that again. Anytime she wanted me whipped, he said—and through the window I could see him buckling his belt with a grim determination as though he meant never to take it off again—she would have to do it herself. Frightened by the effect I had had, I scrubbed my face until it was red. Too late. The dirt I could wash off but not the lines, invisible then but formed, like film exposed and waiting in the camera to be developed, that would come from disappointment and bitterness when my will was thwarted, when my parents were no longer there to indulge my whims and forbear my stubbornness.

True to his vow, my father never whipped me again. My mother did so almost never, often as I deserved it, much as I needed it. Why my parents were so loath to punish me when I was bad, or to correct me when I was unruly, why they spoiled me, with effects that I feel to my sorrow to this day, I was not to learn for many years. If my way to school brought me to it from the rear, as it did when we lived on Third Street, then it took me past the scenes of two of the accidents of my life: the vacant lot where I got the hurt which so terrified my mother and which kept me in bed all one summer; and then the gully down behind the playground where, one day when I was ten, I sprained my right ankle for the first of many times, and through this learned the secret of my birth (or one of them), carefully kept from me until then, why I had been so slow to walk and why in all my baby pictures I have got only one leg—the right one tucked out of sight beneath my dress—why in all of them I am reaching out, wanting to be picked up or unable to get to whatever has attracted me and reaching out for it, why my mother had never given me the baby brother or sister that had been my Christmas wish every year that I could remember, and of the guilt and self-reproach over me that she had lived with all my life.

THERE WAS NO COLLEGE in Clarksville and, strictly speaking, there never had been; but there was a College Avenue, so named because, if pursued about five miles out into the country, it led to the ruins of the Clarksville Female Academy, defunct since 1848. If the long climb up College Avenue was my way to school, then I had company on my walk, quite a lot of it before we got there, for I lived down at the foot of the street and the schoolhouse sat up at the top.

Directly across the street from me lived Martin Scaffe. Whichever of us was ready first waited for the other one and we set off for school together. I was fond of Martin: a gentle, good-natured, smart and lively-minded boy, and yet something—something on my side —kept us from being the very best of friends. Because he was the only boy I had ever known whose father was dead, I felt ill at ease with Martin. His loss made him pitiable, and I did pity him, but it also made him different, and toward anyone different I felt a certain fear, and a certain defensiveness. I tried to put myself in Martin's place and imagine how I would feel without my father, and I could imagine just enough of how he must feel to dislike putting myself in his place, while at the same time being able to imagine so little of Martin's feelings as to be bewildered and frightened.

Martin was a reminder of that most terrifying of all things to a child: the extent to which life is shaped by accident, of how suddenly the unforeseen can strike and change everything. Only a short time ago Martin was just like me, just like all us boys. His father had only recently died. Thus, inside Martin's house still hung a hush of mourning. This made his house a gloomy and forbidding one to me. Mr. Scaffe had died young, full of health, and having just achieved great success, while waiting to assume the high county office to which he had been elected. Martin's mother, herself a lawyer, had assumed the office to which her husband had been elected. So, things could have been worse for Martin— would certainly have been worse for any other boy in town, for Mrs. Scaffe was the only professional woman, aside from schoolteachers, in all of Red River County at that period. And yet I could not imagine anything worse than losing one of your parents. I could not imagine it, it was so terrible. To me it was a wonder that Martin could bring himself to go to school, study, play, be a normal boy. Plainly, his bereavement had sobered him, aged him beyond his years. He now had a quietness and a seriousness of mind that the rest of us boys lacked. He was more thoughtful of his mother, and refused to go along with us on adventures which might worry her. Sometimes his maturity shamed me for my frivolousness.

Waiting for Martin and me on the first corner up the street would be Jimmy Kelty. Jimmy, too, knew what trouble in the family was. His older sister, Cleo, had been confined all her life in bed, indeed, was strapped to a wooden board, immobile, and would be for however long she lived, afflicted with tuberculosis of the spine. She was the only person anywhere near my own age to whom I had ever heard applied the terrible words, "She would be better off dead." It was a duty we children of the neighborhood felt, or were made by our mothers to feel, to pay an occasional visit to Cleo. Like all normal, healthy, selfish children, I felt more distaste than compassion for the abnormal, the unhealthy, and saw them as a standing threat to my own good luck. I always dreaded my visits to Cleo Kelty, always came away terrified and disgusted by the sight of the poor thing who had never known what it was to be a child, would never know what it was to be a grownup.

Just up the block, Martin, Jimmy and I would be joined by Bobby Williams. Chubby, sunny, easygoing Bobby was one of the smartest boys in our class. I envied Bobby, but not for that. I envied him because he did not have to prove all the time that he was smart, as I did. Son of a judge and of a mother from one of the town's solid old families, not one like mine trying to climb the social ladder starting on the lowest rung, Bobby was also blessed with a brother. He was not his parents' only hope.

At the next corner we would be joined by Sammy Harris, but although Sammy was one of the liveliest boys of our group, his joining us on the way to school did not much enliven us. This was because at his corner we were also joined by Miss Ella Watson, our principal and our fifth-grade teacher.

Walking behind Miss Ella you felt as you feel when out driving you find yourself behind a hearse: you wish you could pass but propriety forbids.

Miss Ella could bend, or break, in two places, to sit, at right angles, like a carpenter's folding rule. She was as angular as a step when she folded herself into a chair, as plumb as a wall when she stood. This was called "posture" in those days, and the opposite of it was called "slumping" when seated, "slouching" when erect.

Neither slouching nor slumping was tolerated at Clarksville Grammar School. After Miss Ella's frosty "Good
morning" to us—her face, like her dress, had as much
variety, day to day, as a statue's—we stiffened ourselves
and fell in behind her, keeping order as if she had eyes
in the back of her head (as we half believed she had)
the rest of the way to school.

Best of all my many different walks to school were
those that took me clear across town, and the best of
these was the one during the time which to this day I
still call to myself "When we lived behind the Grigsbys,"
or, as a variation on that, one which fines it down still
closer to the special place in my affections that that
house and that period have for me—and that one was
the only house I ever cried on leaving—"The time we
lived behind Miss Belle."

She was not "Miss" Belle at all, but such were the
inconsistencies of female titles of address among us—
we had aunties who were only-children and never knew
a nephew or a niece, grannies who had never borne a
child, one woman who went through life as Miss Jane
while another was Miss Jones—that nobody thought it
strange that Mrs. Grigsby, long married, mother of a
married daughter (but not a grandmother, and that is
where I come in), should be "Miss" Belle. Perhaps she
had been Miss Belle for so long before becoming Mrs.
Grigsby that it was easier for people to get used to a new
last name for her than a new first one.

My moving into the house behind her back fence rea-
woke in Miss Belle a long-neglected talent for baking
cookies and making candies and frying doughnuts. Her

kitchen, at the rear of her house, was just over the board fence at our back door, and on Saturday mornings my appetite for a balanced breakfast would be spoiled by the sugared smells already wafting our way. In mid morning our phone would ring—Miss Belle was much too refined to shout over her back fence—and she would ask if I would like to come over. In expectation of this call, my mother would have me scrubbed, curried and polished almost as neat as for another schoolday. So certain was there to be a last-minute speck of dirt somewhere on my face, something which only a mother could see, that I handed her my handkerchief before she could ask me for it, she wet a corner of it on her tongue, and scrubbed the spot off while catechizing me on my manners. On leaving the house to go outdoors, I always had a spot somewhere on my face where the skin was stiff from my mother's dried spit. "Now see that you behave yourself and don't mortify me," she said. "Don't tire Miss Belle. Remember, she is an old woman. You mustn't ask her to be always making things for you the way you do me—she's not your mother, you know. And remember, cur'osity killed the cat, so keep down that idle cur'osity of yours" (she always called it my "idle cur'osity," which once occasioned my father's saying, "Idle curiosity hell. He's got the hardest-working curiosity I ever came across") "and don't pester the life out of her with your questions. Don't wear out your welcome. Come home without me having to telephone for you. *And*" (this command was given emphasis and valedictory position because my mother knew my awful itch to open drawers and peek behind closed doors in other people's houses, to her the worst breach of etiquette a child could commit) *"don't meddle!"*

Throughout the rest of the day, Miss Belle's telephone would ring from time to time, and if I was within earshot, if, for instance, she was giving me a fitting of whatever costume I had her sewing, required by my weekly change of mind about what I really wanted to be —pilot, pirate, policeman, Indian—I would hear her say, "Well, of course, if you insist, Nell. But, believe me, he's no trouble to me. He's company for me. He keeps himself occupied. And he does seem to be having such a good time." With Miss Belle's blessing, what I kept myself occupied with was quietly, intently meddling. No closet of all the many in her big old house, where three generations of her family had lived, was closed to me, none did I leave unemptied in the course of that time, when even Saturday down on the square lost its lure for me.

Nobody in my family, big as it was, lived in a house with an attic, or had ever lived in any one house long enough to store much in an attic if there had been one. Of my great-grandparents, only four of the eight ever made it to Texas (there was reason to believe that one of those, instead of coming there, had, along with whatever tribe he was of, always been there, though living not in a house but in a tepee—again, no attic; in any case, he had died leaving nothing to his name). To have an attic, and it full of family mementoes, was to me a mark of superior birth, that was what was meant by "background," and when I was not rummaging among Miss Belle's trove of relics, I was quizzing her about something I had dug out, gathering lore about her ancestors as though I was adopting them to take the place of those I myself lacked. Many of those old photographs and keepsakes, quaint old clothes, newspaper clippings, playbills from Clarksville's defunct old Trilling Opera House, packed away long ago and not until by me brought back to the light of day, brought back to Miss Belle memories long in storage in her mind, and tales associated with them which she enjoyed telling me as much as I enjoyed hearing them. Once I came down from her attic with a quirt, like the one carried by that gay gaucho Douglas Fairbanks, and just from the look on my face Miss Belle said, "Now there is something that I don't have any use for, and neither, I'm sure, has Newt [her husband]. You take that—" thereby earning herself an order for a new costume, size 8 short, to go with it.

When that was the house that I set off from for school, then my companion on my walk, as far as the square, was Mr. Grigsby. He would wait for me on his front porch and I would come around to pick him up and we walked together the four blocks from his house downtown. He with his briefcase, I with my satchel, together we looked like very senior and very junior partners in business. For, be it understood, when I set off for school in the morning it was not in the blue jeans, dungarees, chinos, knits of a later generation; when I set off for school it was in a suit—blue serge in cool weather, white linen in warm: a single-breasted jacket, short pants creased to a cutting edge, knee-high stockings, a shirt with a starched collar and a necktie, freshly polished shoes. So did the other schoolboys of Clarksville of my day, though not all were sent back after lunch, as I was on hot days, re-bathed and in a fresh white linen suit. Except for the necktie and the socks, none of this was store-bought; my shirts, my suits were custom-tailored for me by my mother. Mr. Grigsby was not a talkative man; I felt I gained stature with grown men by not prattling. Of course, when he had some question that I could answer for him, I obliged.

To be present at the hub of things each morning when the town woke, counted the chimes of its clock, rubbed its eyes, yawned, stretched and fell to work at its many trades, was to be alive. The square would be just opening for business when I bade Mr. Grigsby goodbye and made my way through it, and right here is as good a place as any to explode a myth: that of the lazy, inefficient and shiftless Southerner—one of the most misleading myths I have ever met with, so much so that it must be deliberate, spread by the rascal himself, whose guile matches his drive, in hopes of deceiving Yankees into thinking he is unambitious and easily outsmarted, stupefied by his climate and too debilitated by hookworm to go to his mailbox and tote back his welfare check. More energetic and industrious people do not exist, unless it be the Japanese—a trait of theirs long recognized and exploited by mill and factory owners, both resident and absentee. Clarksville, during a depression, and under its own special curbs of drought and dust storms, was a hive of activity from early morning until night—even in the heat of summer, which made the place a kiln (and summer there was eight months of the year) with temperatures already in May that you would think only a salamander could survive in, but which only made the natives work the harder, as do the damned when the heat goes up in Hell.

True, the lunch hour on those breathless days was a bit prolonged, but it was never allowed to stretch into a siesta. Back went I and all the other schoolchildren through that heat to our classrooms on time. I never knew a boy or a girl to take an afternoon nap unless he or she was seriously sick. The tolling of one o'clock by the courthouse clock was the opening note in a symphony of sounds that recommenced on cue from every shop. And this was the era when the only relief from the heat was the electric fan, long before air conditioning was introduced even at the picture-show, which in any case ran in the daytime only on Saturday, as nobody could take time off for a matinee. Mr. Kirksey, the blacksmith, did not moderate the music from his anvil just because the air around him was as hot as his forge, nor did the hammering from that other shop around the corner from his which represented the other mode of transportation, and all that could go wrong with it, I mean my father's garage, take time out to wait for a cool spell or a shower. From May to October, sunstroke was certain for anybody who ventured out of doors as far as his or her garden gate without a broad-brimmed straw hat, and you really got to see people unshaded only in wintertime, as the limbs of trees can be seen only after the leaves are off. The bowl of the square in Clarksville, at noontime, spring, summer and fall, was as hot as the interior of a skillet, and people standing there seemed not to be sweating but frying like sausages. But work went on, beginning early and lasting late.

The square had an air of permanence which the tolling of the clock only enforced; for Clarksville was an old, old town—older even than the books said. Nothing like as old as the Spanish towns of south Texas, but of the Protestant towns, the oldest. 1820, the books gave as the date of its founding, but freebooters and squatters, runaway slaves and other fugitives, people of the sort not to advertise their whereabouts, were there a generation before that. They were there to greet Stephen F. Austin's American colonists. For a long time the town was an outpost all alone. On the 1840 edition of Austin's map of the State, or rather, the Republic, you will search in vain for Dallas, Fort Worth, Houston, or, indeed, any other city or town for two hundred miles south of Clarksville or west of it all the way to Santa Fe.

Since then, Clarksville had changed little; now change had come, and, fuelled by internal combustion, the pace accelerated daily. It was to be noted in sights and sounds, in the way people dressed. Young as I was, I had witnessed the quickening in tempo. Formerly the square in the morning rumbled with iron-bound wheels on its wooden paving bricks, the clop of hooves, the groan of wooden axles and the creak of wagonbeds. These sounds were still to be heard, but more rarely. They were giving way to the whop of pneumatic tires, the throb of engines, the bleat of horns. The costume suited to the wagon, ground-length dresses and poke-bonnets, was not often seen any more. There was a new caution. "Be careful crossing the street," a recent admonition, was heard more and more nowadays.

OF ALL MY MANY WAYS to school, only one did I ever dread. Not because it took me through the cemetery (where, beneath the ground I once played on, I shall one day lie); that held no terrors, nor any sorrows— no loved ones—for me, although if one wanted to scare himself with ghosts, then the old cemetery in Clarksville had a better claim than most to be haunted by bloody and vengeful ones, for on the street at its edge, interrupting its iron rail fence, stood the great oak known as the Hanging Tree, or Page's Tree, after a pioneering murderer of that name, the first of many outlaws to meet rough justice at the hands of vigilantes on the limb that overhung my walk. But on those mornings when the chimes of Old Red warned me that I was falling behind time, and must risk either the lane down behind the cemetery or a demerit for tardiness from Miss Ella Watson, then I chose the shortcut through the cemetery and the lane.

The lane was short, quickly traversed, and in my passage through it I looked straight ahead of me, both to spare myself the sight and to avoid rousing the hostility of the inhabitants, which was easily roused, for, like all of their class, they were suspicious-minded and hypersensitive to the nosiness of strangers, especially neatly dressed, studious-looking little boy strangers. Still, I saw enough for the place and the people who lived there to symbolize something for me, something I both feared and despised. The houses were old, rickety, unpainted, too small for the families that teemed in them. As a result, life there was lived as much outdoors as in, as is the life of animals, between the barn and the barnlot. On the front porches were furnishings that belonged inside—if not in the weed-grown and eroded gully which I would yet have to scramble through, where the denizens of the lane threw old bedsprings, bottles, battered chamberpots: a discarded icebox too heavy to be toted any farther, a sagging settee, its cotton entrails hanging out. Broken windowpanes were stuffed temporarily with rags, left there permanently. The smell of privies was pervasive. From every clothesline hung dingy diapers. In more than one front yard rested the hull of an old car, the playhouse for a litter of ragged, sometimes bare-bottomed, towheaded, snotnosed kids, whose mothers' supervision over them was incessant, shrill, foul-mouthed, ferocious and ineffectual. Such squalor and brutishness embarrassed and offended me. It distressed me. My mother, too. These were not even the sort of people she called "common"; these were the sort she called "trash." One lowered oneself by talking about them. And so my mother and I avoided the subject.

MANY AS WERE THE WAYS to school that my residence in different parts of town over the years took me, there was one that was never mine. The street which had been called Silk Stocking Street for so long that everybody had forgotten its real name was one of the two parts of Clarksville that I knew only as a tourist, the other being Niggertown. On Silk Stocking Street, in their huge houses built with the ponderous playfulness of the 1880's, in a style combining elements of the Kremlin, Brighton Pavilion and the Taj Mahal, lived the Marables, the McCullochs, the Dinwiddies, and the other first families of the town. Many of these had once owned slaves; now, each morning from out of Niggertown, strung along the creek north of the jailhouse, descendants of those slaves, many of them with the same names as their employers, trooped up Silk Stocking Street to work in and around the houses as cooks, house-maids and yard men—or, as we said, "boys."

Honeysuckle, roses, wisteria, magnolia blossoms perfumed—sometimes nearly stifled—Silk Stocking Street. Silver globes the size of basketballs on stone pedestals ornamented the carpeted lawns. Carriage houses, some of them bigger than the house itself, stood behind the houses. Garages now. Although from his, behind his mansion—for so it seemed to us—Mr. "Red" Robbins, the town's leading lawyer (he who once said to my father, " 'Ump, you hot-tempered little devil, if you ever want to kill some sonofabitch, see me about it first, hear?"), still rode his sorrel saddlehorse downtown every morning, stabling it for the day in Cliff Adams's livery stable in the back lane of the north block of the square.

JUST AS THERE WAS ONE WAY to school that I often wished was mine, and knew in my bones never would be, so too there was, or had once been, one house I had lived in that I should have liked to pass on my way there, but never would. This vanished house, as different from all other houses in Clarksville as my father was different from all other fathers, assumed in my mind the exaggerated importance of something one has lost and knows that to search for is futile, and yet for that very reason is something one cannot give up hope of finding. I even indulged myself in daydreams that perhaps my mother was mistaken in saying it was no longer there, and that I would still discover it someday—just as, for years afterwards, I used to dream regularly that my father had come back, explaining that he had had to go away, to disappear for a while, and apologizing for having tricked me and given me such a bad scare. It is said that people who have never known one or both of their parents nor who they were are piqued by curiosity about them all their lives, and that there is even an organization of these adult orphans who assist one another in their search for their lost mothers and fathers, or for any scrap of knowledge about them; I can well understand that urge: I felt something akin to it about the house I was born in, and which had been torn down shortly after my birth. My longing for this nonexistent house, instead of lessening as I got older and presumably more sensible, actually grew; for it ceased to be a longing for a house and became a longing for a state of being which the house had come to symbolize for me. We retreat from unhappiness as far as our experience, or our imagination, allows us to go. As relations between my mother and father began to go bad—or as I, with expanding consciousness, became aware that they had—and would periodically poison the atmosphere of our house, I turned in my imagination to the time when we were just starting life together, when, in the words of that favorite song of my songbird of a mother, we, just Molly and me, and Baby makes three, were happy in our blue heaven—not knowing that that had been the most difficult time we had ever had, especially me. I did know that that house, their first, was also the first one to which he ever came home to her drunk; but she had not minded then, as an anecdote—the only one I knew relating to that house, one that she told me before it stopped being funny—showed. If she accused him of having been drinking when he came home late that night, it was because she thought it her duty to me, to herself and to him now that they had me, and because she owed it to her mother's upbringing, to remonstrate when she smelled liquor on her husband's breath. He expressed the astonishment and indignation which this preposterous charge always elicits. But when he went to wash his face to show how sober he was, he stripped naked. Except for his felt hat. And when he had washed his face and took the washpan to the window and flung out the water, the window was down. His drinking was comical then, like the clowns in the silent one-reelers of the period. It might make him quarrelsome with other men, at dances, on the square on Saturday nights, but she was not averse to his picking quarrels with men over real or fancied attentions paid to her. The surliness, the violence at home, would come later.

I did not even know where in Clarksville the house I was born in had stood, for, from her unwillingness to talk about it, I sensed that to my mother, as to me, the destruction of that house was saddening, and so I did not pester her. After that house which I never knew was joined by the one whose destruction I had endured, in which I lost all my toys, my keepsakes, all our family photographs except for the few that relatives had other prints of, in which were burned all the mementoes of my first ten years—links to one's former selves, saved in order to connect our stages (larva, pupa, chrysalis) into one continuous growth, in a vain effort to go into the grave intact, one person—I mourned for it still more.

WHEN THE MOOD WAS UPON ME (and the troubles between my mother and father brought it more frequently) I ached for a brother or a sister as for a sweetheart. I coaxed my mother, not knowing how painful this was to her, to hurry and give me one before I got too much older than he or she. How I envied those of my friends who had one! How it shamed and angered me when they teased theirs or would not let them play with us older boys and chased them home crying their little hearts out. I would never do that to mine. As a big brother I would have been as proud as a parent. I would have loved to guide my little brother or sister around town, show him or her all the discoveries I had made for myself, and show him or her off to everybody I knew. I would have loved to help him or her with homework. It would have doubled my pleasures to have someone to share them with, it would have halved my sorrows to have someone to share them with me.

Of course, at the same time, I thoroughly enjoyed being the sole object of my parents' attention, affection and indulgence, and would certainly have resented sharing them. I thought I could have a brother or a sister without sharing my parents with him or her. I was, in equal parts, both selfish and lonely. Every only child is Narcissus—that other Narcissus of whom Pausanias tells us, pining not for himself but for his lost twin, the cure for his congenital, lifelong loneliness.

I WAS LIKE A TEMPERAMENTAL WATCH, except that my irregularities were regular: I ran slow all week—all winter—fast on Saturdays—all summer. On schooldays my mother had to shake me awake; on Saturdays I was up before the sun was, and even before breakfast was ready, I had a fire going under the cast-iron washpot in whatever back yard was ours at the time and the water in it already beginning to steam, ready for the laundress —my one chore, one I liked—before I was free to go and play. Schooldays, it almost took a fire under me to get me up.

Unless it happened to be a semester when my way to school took me past the home of the girl I was in love with; and then—if she let me—I was there on time to carry her satchel. People speak of a "sickly" child; I was a lovesickly child. When I started school, aged six, I fell in love on the first day—maybe with the first girl; hers was the first name on roll call: Doris Adams, and I loved her to distraction, was faithful to her for years— two, at least. It really was an illness with me, chronic, incurable, with all the symptoms: mooniness, loss of appetite, a heart that was swollen and tender all the time, breath I could seldom draw without a catch. Though the world was full of budding, blossoming and full-blown girls, I had no eyes for them, no more than a wren has for a robin. It was those my own age who drew me. Nothing in life was so beautiful to me as a flat-chested, snaggle-toothed little girl. I was in love with every one of them in my grade all through grammar school, and not by turns: I never really fell out of love with any of them, I just for the time being loved one more than the generality. I would look up from my desk and catch sight of a girl I had known all my life and it would be as though I had never seen her before. What was the matter with me? How on earth had I let eleven whole years of my life waste away without realizing how madly I loved Mildred Wooley? How could I wait until recess to tell her so? How would I live over it if she spurned me?

However, I looked up from my desk only rarely. For once we had lined up alphabetically and answered the roll call and marched into the schoolhouse, it was work —for me, war.

All through grammar school I was an A student in every subject. In Deportment, too: A+ — a studious and well-behaved boy. At the end of the first year I had been double-promoted: skipped over Low Second grade and put into High Second. I had been almost as proud of myself as my mother was of me. I did not know the main cause of her satisfaction. I did not know what I had gotten into. I soon learned.

In my new class—and I would go through the rest of my schooling in that same class—only one pupil rivaled me. This was Billy Barton, and he rivaled me all too closely. In fact, about half the time Billy's report card averaged a fraction of a letter better than mine. On those occasions my homeward steps lagged heavily. My mother could not bear for me to be excelled by anybody; it was a draught of gall for her when Billy Barton did. There was no chance that she might not learn of Billy's having excelled me (the same was true, in reverse, in Billy's case), for his father was the Barton, mine the Humphrey, of *Barton & Humphrey's Garage.*

Between Billy Barton and me our teachers all maintained a strict neutrality. Miss Ella Watson was neutral by nature—not one ever to have a teacher's pet. Even at the end of our year under her, Mrs. Sea (she was a widow) probably did not know one Billy from the other; children were not people to her, they were her job, and one she disliked. Miss Addie Dinwiddie seemed to know that she would be caught between a tigress (my mother) and a she-bear (Billy's) if she should favor the cub of one over that of the other. Result: she was impartially severe on us both.

The cut that Mrs. Barton suffered when I was double-promoted into her Billy's class never healed. She herself picked at the scab. My mother helped her by continually rubbing salt in the wound. Later, when the partnership between Barton and Humphrey dissolved in acid, it was even more imperative that I excel Billy at school.

So far as Billy and I were concerned, there was nothing personal in the rivalry between us. He and I were not volunteers, we were draftees in the war between us. We did not fraternize, yet we respected and even mutely sympathized with each other. Across the battle-field of scarred and pitted desks as, during the daily spelling bee, we, the last of either side left standing, fired words machine-gunlike at each other; through the haze of chalk dust; in the dread hush of final exams, broken only by the scurrying of pencils on paper, Billy Barton and I would sometimes exchange a look of mutual recognition and mutual helplessness, even such a look as two foot soldiers might exchange across no-man's-land before lobbing their grenades: "Nothing personal, you understand, but it's either you or me."

But it was not only Billy Barton I was in competition with. What spurred me and made me studious and ambitious was insecurity and fear—insecurity about my origins, fear of the times. They were also making me into a little prig, a snob, both social and intellectual.

Poverty could claim cousins with me—first cousins. Closer kin than that: grandparents, on both sides. My mother, a would-be social snob, had hoisted herself above her beginnings, pushing me ahead of her, but the bank up which she had climbed was steep and slippery, and from where we had gotten you could still see the bottom of the gulch. She had the respect for learning that the uneducated have, and, as they all do, she saw it not as a reward in itself but as a means of advancement. Knowing no better, I then saw it that way, too. My mother was determined that within two generations, hers and mine, the evolution of the species Humphrey would be completed. That she ran the risk of teaching me to look down upon her as a lower form had not occurred to her.

She had already declared our branch a distinct genus. There was a difference in the family, and it occasioned quarrels, some of them heated, over what our name was. Against all those born to it, my mother maintained that it was Humphrey; they claimed it was Humphreys and always had been until she changed it. I had a suspicion that they were right, and another suspicion as to why my mother had changed it. My mother longed to be accepted by the town's better sort of people, and among the rather grossly large clan of Humphreys were some whom she would sooner not be lumped with. In particular, there was that younger brother of my father's now serving time for a badly bungled job of breaking and entering. As everybody in Clarksville and all of Red River County knew everybody else, and could tell you who had married anybody's third cousin's middle step-daughter's oldest boy, I do not know whom my mother thought she was fooling. But anyway, for her, dropping the "s" from the name was like bobbing a bit off the nose, for some people. At least to herself, in the mirror, it was an improvement.

I was aware of our struggle to keep financially afloat —my mother would have said, to stay respectable—and that it was getting harder all the time. Our unfertilized finances went through regular monthly cramps. Everything we owned was really owned by one or another finance company; we were buying it all on the installment plan—we and fifty million other American families in the 1930's. The car, the kitchen range, the refrigerator, the radio: with each the purchaser got a coupon book. These coupons were dated monthly, stretching into the years, to be clipped out and sent in by mail, remittance enclosed. Fall behind in your payment for three installments, the appliance was repossessed and all hope of ever again buying anything was lost; your credit rating was ruined, and you along with it. The interest rates charged were usurious, the term of credit adjusted like a time-bomb to the working life of the appliance, so that the final payment on one coincided with the down payment on its replacement. Most nights it was I doing my figures on the porcelainized kitchen tabletop, struggling with my huge assignment of homework; on the eve of the first of the month it was my parents, and their difficulties with their accounts erased the difference in our ages. Having paid all the coupons, they then added up Mr. Pritchard, the butcher's bill, Mr. Raines, the grocer's bill, and the bill from the filling station and the gas company and the water company and the rent, if we were paying rent, the premium for the insurance on my father's life. They "posted" bills to my father's customers, more and more of whom were falling into arrears. In trying that night to cope with their "books," to get satisfaction from their debtors and to satisfy their creditors, my parents were reduced to the same anxiety I faced nightly with my homework. As I had gone further in school than either of them, than both of them, they often turned to me for help with their arithmetic. This embarrassed me for their sakes and made me feel ashamed—whether ashamed of them or ashamed of myself for feeling ashamed of them, I could not have said.

It may not be a burdensome thing to be a child better educated than one's parents if the difference is, say, between a PhD and a master's degree. But when a ten-year-old in the fifth grade of grammar school has already had as much schooling as his father and mother put together, an odd and unsettling reversal of roles occurs. It fanned in me the spark of rebellion. Here was I, little and forced to take orders from and be scolded by and sometimes, though not often and never severely, punished by people who knew less than I knew already, whom I had to help with their addition and subtraction.

I could see that times were hard, that we were not all that much better off than the folks who lived in the lane down behind the cemetery, and that if I was ever to get where my mother wanted me to go, to live one day in a big house up on Silk Stocking Street, I must study hard and make good grades at school and be a good boy and please my teachers. I did. I was a prize pupil and a model boy. Imagine, then, Miss Ella Watson's amazement when Billy Humphrey's was the hand held up in answer to her question, "Who made that vulgar sound?"

"I did, Miss Ella."

"Billy! Billy Humphrey! You!"

Each exclamation added altitude to the heights from which I had fallen. Hugging her incredulity to me, I crashed upon the rocks of her disillusionment.

"Yes, Ma'am," I murmured.

"Then Billy Humphrey will be kept in for an hour after school. Children, march!"

We filed on down the corridor, I hobbling along in my place among the H's on the balls of my tortured and aching feet, blinking back my tears, trying to hide them both from those who felt my disgrace and from those boys who were so hardened to being kept in after school that to them it was a mark of pride.

This happened as we were returning to class after
lunch hour. I had the rest of the day to brood upon my
downfall, and to prepare myself for the moment when
the news would have to be broken to my mother. This
would have to happen on an afternoon when she was
to pick me up by car to keep an appointment.

I was, as they say, "hard on shoes." My mother used
to sigh and exclaim, "That boy! I declare you scarcely
get home from the store with him before he's gone
through another pair of shoes!" I did wear shoes out
fairly quickly; but when my mother complained to
women friends about how often she had to buy me shoes,
she was really letting them know that when her boy
went off to school in the morning it was in shoes that
were not scuffed.

Now, however, we were deep in the great depression (it was a little late getting to Clarksville—as was
everything) and my mother was economizing in every
way. Casting about for where to begin with me, she
hit upon my shoes. She determined to take them to the
cobbler and have steel taps put on the heels and toes
to save wear. I was appalled at this suggestion, and
doubly appalled that it should come from my mother.
Did she not know what sort of boys wore taps on their
shoes?

Inconspicuousness, which I equated with gentility
and breeding, was a passion of mine, and with a set of
those taps on your shoes you were about as inconspicu-
ous as a sow on a parquet floor. But it was not just the
unwanted attention they drew upon you that prejudiced
me against shoe taps. It would be thought that I actually
liked them. A certain low class of boys, the only sort I
knew who wore them, did. Sullen and subdued enough

through the week at school (which they were only waiting until they were legally of age to drop out from), these
boys used to appear on the square downtown on Saturday afternoons transformed: bold and swaggering,
coarse-mouthed, bullying. Sons for the most part of saw-
mill hands and truckers, they affected already their
fathers' day-off dress: khaki uniforms, black leather
bow-ties, wide belts with big buckles, and on the heels
and toes of their shoes, steel taps of precisely the sort
which my mother now proposed I be shod with, though
in my case the motive was economy and in theirs it was
rather an extravagance. Those boys had a way of sauntering and dragging their feet and scraping their taps
which all but struck sparks on the pavement. Of all the
many little recognition marks of caste which I had
compiled—and I was a walking catalogue of them—
shoe taps were perhaps the most conclusively damning,
worse than long sideburns, or calling a boil a "risin'."

So when Miss Ella asked who had made that vulgar
sound, my hand shot up in almost eager guilt. And when
school let out that afternoon and I asked Miss Ella's
permission to go and tell my mother I was being kept in,
I expected her to be smitten with shame and sorrow
for the humiliation she had brought upon me, and to
offer to serve my sentence herself.

My mother charged from the car and into the schoolhouse with her maternity bristling like a hen partridge,
and within minutes I was free. There had been a mis-
understanding, she told me. The guilty party, she told
me, as my father, at the garage, removed the taps from
my shoes, was some other boy and he had made a different sort of sound. I was some time in figuring out
what kind of sound a boy could make more vulgar than

I with my shoe taps. When I did, I wondered what euphemism decorous enough to pass those prim, pursed lips of hers Miss Ella had found from which it could be learned that while marching to class some boy had let a fart audible even above the tapping of my shoes.

ON MORNINGS when I did not have to go to school I was like a pup let off the leash. My rovings then were off the beaten path. Backalleys, unpaved lanes: no longer were they like the map on the wall at school printed so long ago that the area of present-day Colorado-Utah was labelled "The Great American Desert"—not after my explorations and discoveries. Barn lofts: I knew them all. Living off the land—crawfish tails skewered on a stick and roasted over my campfire—I traced the creek as far as the City Limit signs. I surveyed, I took census, I compiled. Like that other William, Conqueror of England, I catalogued my Domesday Book, listing everything that was mine: people, livestock, land, houses, bodies of water, trees of noteworthy growth.

The livery stable, the blacksmith shop and my father's garage: those, in my time, were a Clarksville boy's downtown rounds when he was out of school on Saturday or on a summer morning. It was better not to come in too large and noisy a group, but singly or in two's and three's, boys—even I, though of the enemy camp—were welcome to sit on the bench against the wall of Cliff Adams's decaying livery stable and listen to the talk of the farmers about crops and hunting, chewing gum and spitting toward the gutter in imitation of their tobacco-chewing. We could look at the horses and bounce on the seat of one of the old buggies, now sagging from disuse. At the blacksmith shop Mr. Kirksey was shoeing fewer horses every year, and surely I reminded him of the reason, but I was as welcome as any other boy to watch him forge a shoe and shoe a horse or rim a wagonwheel. But at that third shop, the one which was inexorably putting the first two out of business, and which for Clarksville boys of my day was the most magnetic shop of all, my father's garage, I was the only boy in town not allowed to hang around. This was not because my father did not love me, but because he did.

It is hard to make understood now the importance that cars had in the life of a boy in my time and place. Not being then nearly as common as now, the automobile had not yet become just a mode of transportation; it was still associated with pioneering men doing deeds as daring as those of the airplane pilots of the day flying solo around the world and discovering the Poles. There were many more makes of cars, and they were more individual. We did not know that many of them would become classics and be treasured in museums like works of art; we did know that they were handsome and powerful, and fast.

If Clarksville had had an airport, no doubt it would have given the garage some competition for boys' interest; it did not, and so they were drawn to the garage. Not one of them but felt a passing ambition at one time or another to be a mechanic, so much more glamorous an occupation than storekeeper or postman or pharmacist. The very griminess of a mechanic made him attractive to a boy.

My father was not unaware of my love of cars; he understood it all too well. He himself loved them—that was why we changed them as often as we did houses:

a new one, a faster one, would take his fancy—he was a Cassanova of cars; and he loved his work (though not the griminess of it, for he was the most fanatically clean man I ever knew): how could a son of his not love them too? But my father wanted something better for his only son than being what he himself called "a greasemonkey," and he was not unhappy, I suspect, over a disability of mine which, although it did not keep me from being a car-lover, made my affair with them Platonic; namely, my chronic carsickness. My father saw himself as a link in a chain, and he took it for granted that I would get as far ahead of him as he had gotten ahead of his father, and with as little help from him. To draw a comparison from the realm of transportation (which was my father's trade), the three modes of it which the three generations represented: the wagon, the automobile, and the airplane: the automobile had empowered my father to leave the farm—he wanted me to fly.

Thus it was that I, envied by my friends for my nearness to one of those romantic figures, a mechanic, was the one boy in town not allowed to hang around the garage and soak up the talk of magnetos and carburetors and cut-outs, and be asked, joy of joys, by the black-faced man lying on his dolly underneath a car to hand him a certain wrench. Unlike many boys, who expect to join their fathers in business, my relations with mine were strictly for pleasure. He never talked shop with me. Whenever I asked my father what kind of car was the one that had just passed, a question which absorbed every boy, when we collected car-sightings as avidly as bird-watchers collect birds and gained stature with our friends when we could claim having seen an Auburn or a Marmon or some other exotic marque, he sometimes pretended not to have been looking. Finally some of his sense of inferiority about being a "greasemonkey" wore off on me, to the extent that whenever I was with a friend on the square and a car came through with my father lying on the hood of it listening to the beat of the engine to diagnose what ailed it, I did not know whether not to notice him, or to swell with pride.

Over the years the garage had become even more of a local attraction—an attraction of a different sort, and for people other than just boys.

Cars kept multiplying like maggots, and the new models each year sported speedometers with maximum speeds ten miles per hour faster. I remember the wonder with which we first breathed the phrase, "A mile a minute!" I remember the first one I ever saw with a speedometer that went up to 100, and how we gaped at it in awe and admiration.

As cars proliferated and their speeds increased, car accidents multiplied. My father saw in this ever-growing number of wrecks an opportunity to make money. No longer did cars require only a mechanic to keep them running; all the accidents had created a new trade: the body repairman. This trade my father taught himself. He had to keep up with the times.

With swages and dollies and an assortment of odd-shaped hammers, he beat out the dents in fenders and cabs. He learned to spray on the lacquer and to sand and smooth down the coats. Then he practiced until he learned the art of striping. In those days all cars were striped. Not lavishly striped like the custom creations of today's car nuts, but lightly and discreetly striped: a pair of lines running parallel around the window frames, a single one, like the piping on a jacket, around the fender edges—a leftover from the not-so-distant days of the horse-drawn carriage. Little flat sable brushes with slanted tips were used in this work. A hand as steady, a stroke as swift and sure as a surgeon's were demanded. Hundreds of hours of practice, every spare moment he got, went into it before my father acquired the skill. As cars and their speeds kept increasing, and the accidents kept multiplying, it was soon a major part of his work.

And so the garage became a new sort of attraction. Whenever there was a bad accident anywhere in the county, morbid curiosity drew crowds there to see the wreck. That bridling of my enthusiasm for cars which my father had always encouraged, I now began to feel. I began to think of his garage as a kind of hospital annex —sometimes a morgue's.

Now, WHEN I TRY to call to mind my father's father, I can see him clearly enough, but the background surrounding him is vague, or rather, composite, made up of the many places he stayed on over the years. For it is not a memory of my father's homeplace, the old family farmstead, that I have. The family owned no such place. My grandparents moved just about every other fall, going from one farm to another almost as often as we moved from house to house in town. My father's father was a sharecropper. He would contract with a landowner to farm on shares, fifty-fifty, by the year. When his disappointing crop was gathered, they would pack their few belongings in the wagon and hitch the team to it and move a few miles, always in a radius around the tiny settlement of Lone Star, to another place which, next fall, would prove just as unyielding. To the end, going blind with cataracts and feeling his way with his feet in the furrows, my grandfather clung to his dream of gathering a good enough crop for a couple of years in succession to make a down payment on a place of his own and "work for himself." Instead, the gathering of his crop and its sale, the one time of the year when he held cash money in his hand, often left him in debt to the owner of the crossroads store for what he had advanced them to keep alive on.

He was a one-crop farmer, because the old dream died hard that in that one crop—cotton—money was to be made as in none other, although it was that crop itself, unrotated for years, which had bled the land dry. Cotton—twenty to thirty acres of it farmed with hand tools—is a man-killing crop. As soon as the land is dry enough to be worked in the spring, it must be broken with the plow. Already the days are long and hot, and the ground is soon baked brick-hard. The plowshare must be pointed and held in the ground while the horse or the mule strains at the traces. Then the seed are sown and the furrows turned to cover them. When the plants are about a foot high they must be thinned with a hoe, every other one being chopped out. If the spring rains do not wash them out or a dry spell wither them, they will be in boll just in time for the boll weevil to feast on your labor. Picking time comes in late August, early September. You strap on knee-pads and a long sack of cotton duck and you are in the field stooping and crawl-ing and pulling that sack after you before daybreak, out until dark, beneath a searing sun. After just one day of it you cannot straighten your back at night to lie in bed, and your hands, even your work-hardened hands, are raw and bleeding from the sharp-pointed hulls. If your crop is good then so is everybody else's and the price therefore is bad. And when you have gathered it and taken it to the gin and baled it, you turn over half of it to the man who owns the land.

The houses my father's parents were given to live in on the farms they sharecropped were seldom better than shacks, never as sound as the barn. Leaves from the mail-order catalogues papered the single walls and through the cracks in the boards the winter winds blew strong enough to make the coal-oil lamp smoke its chimney. In one that I remember, the floors of the two rooms were dirt—when it rained, mud. They never had window or door screens, and in the summertime, when, even after the sun had set, the close little hut was blazing and breathless and the windows could not be closed, mosquitoes and moths came in in clouds. The mosquitoes were malarial—both my grandfather and my father suffered chronically from fevers and chills, with occasional acute and devastating attacks—and so it was necessary to drape the beds with "bars." Of these details, however, I speak from little acquaintance, for I slept overnight in my grandparents' house few times. The place was too small, too cramped, their provisions too scanty, the atmosphere too uninviting. We visited them out of a sense of duty—my mother's sense of duty, not my father's. Had it been up to him we would never have visited his parents.

It was from the prospect of a life like his father's that my father had fled the farm and come into town. His older brother had already escaped before him, stopped finally by a bullet in his leg in France, and returning no nearer home than Dallas. His younger brother would soon follow, and would be kept from coming home, much as he might have wished to then, by prison bars, leaving Will Humphrey with nobody to help him work the land.

My father's birth and coming of age was coincident with that of the automobile. He was born in the year of the first ones and he came to manhood as they began to be mass-produced. It was the auto's age of innocence. It had not become the monster it has become for us.

Texans took to the automobile with an enthusiasm even exceeding that of the rest of the nation. They had long distances to cover to get anywhere; to this need the mass-produced, inexpensive ("$490 f.o.b. Detroit," as the billboards said), individually owned auto was the answer. And they had land which, so long as the weather was dry, hardly needed paving to be passable, and had been graded by the hand of God. That they began early on to kill themselves and others in them did not dampen their enthusiasm.

An auto was, even more than his pocketwatch, the most complicated mechanism ever to be used by the average early owner—a thing of elaborate intricacy and of frequent breakdowns, and he, the motorist, stood in the same awe of a man able to diagnose what was wrong with it and get it running again as he did of his doctor.

If he had an intuitive understanding of its complicated workings, then this new, valuable and temperamental toy was the way for a lad with two years of one-room country schooling to escape from the drudgery of the farm, the slavery of sharecropping, and make a life for himself in town. My father had that native gift. His fame as a shade-tree mechanic, a wizard, an automobile prodigy, spread, and by the time he was seventeen years old, using what farm tools he could adapt to his needs, he was repairing cars for people from miles around, taking in pay whatever they were pleased to give him. He could fix anything wrong with one of them long before he had the opportunity, except to test it, to drive one. When he began doing that, then along with the gift for repairing them came a zest for driving them as fast as they would go.

III

ALWAYS BEFORE—and there were many times—when I had seen day break, it was in the company of my father. Different as those mornings were from this one now on the grounds of the Paris hospital, with him lying, perhaps at that very moment dying, inside in the emergency room, there was one element—there was the element—to relate it to those other daybreaks I had seen: squirrels. Coming out to feed on the grounds and finding us there at their hour, they barked and scolded as though in me they recognized an old enemy of their kind, son of a veritable scourge of theirs. So I was, and so he was. Not far away, in the window of the taxidermist's shop in downtown Paris, was displayed, and had been for as long as I could remember, a pair of stuffed squirrels, one white, the other black, with a card between them that read: "Shot by Clarence Humphrey, Clarksville." For one hunter to find, even in a long lifetime, both an albino squirrel and one in the even rarer melanistic state, meant shooting a lot of squirrels. On the day he lay fighting for his life in the Paris hospital, my father was just thirty-eight. And I, though just thirteen, had done more hunting than most men of thirty-eight. My father had bought me my first gun, a .22 rifle, and taught me to shoot it when I was still too little to hold it up without a prop. He was my prop, squatting and resting the barrel on his shoulder while I fired.

On those mornings I would be wakened not much later—an hour or an hour and a half—than I had been today. Then I was easily wakened. No need to shake me then. I would have gone to bed early the evening before, early enough to compensate for the trouble I would have, in my excitement, falling asleep. For although I was an old hand at it now, I was still excited on the eve of going hunting with Daddy in the morning.

We would have packed our hunting coats—mine was getting to be almost as shabby, shapeless, patched, blood-stained, and thus more precious to me, as his was—with our lunches the evening before. By lamplight in the living room we put on our union-suits and our old hunting clothes, our tennis shoes, took our guns and stole out of the house. My father would have left the car parked down the block so as not to wake my mother when we started it.

Instinctively as a homing pigeon, my father headed southwest, out the Mt. Vernon road, the one with the sharp curve a short distance out of town, which, in coming the opposite direction on the night of July 4, 1937, he would not complete. How far we went before stopping would depend upon my age at the time: to Claphand Creek, Scatter Creek, Cut Hand Creek, Whiteoak Creek —each one deeper than the last inside Sulphur Bottom. Those sloughs and bayous had been like grades in school to me. Like grades in grammar school, and, just as I would go to high school in the fall, so when my schooling in the woods resumed then, I was to have been taken down to where those creeks all led: big Sulphur River itself—my tutor the man who had once gone into that pathless wilderness after a specimen of the world's rarest and most dangerous game, and brought it out alive.

His own tutor, he too had gone to school in those woods. It was almost all the education he had received.

. . .

Two YEARS in Lone Star's one-room schoolhouse completed the boy's indoor schooling. Two short years, for even at seven and eight, boys were needed at home early in the spring and late into the fall to help with the crops. Two years was enough—more than many children got. He had learned to read a little and to reckon a little— enough to do all the reading and to count all the money that the life marked out for him would bring him.

He was nine going on ten that spring when he was first put to doing a man's work. The year was 1908. It might as well have been 1808; nothing in life had changed in Red River County, Texas, in those hundred years, not for farmfolks like the Humphreys. Within the next ten years everything was to change, and Clarence Humphrey would be one of those to bring this about; but in 1908 plowing was still done as it had always been, behind a mule, and travel was still by wagon over dirt roads. An idea of the boy's size at that age can be had from the fact that fifteen years later, a bridegroom, he stood five feet three and weighed 110. At nine, to plow, he reached up, not down, to the handles.

The Humphreys were a tribe of pygmies. My father's mother, Nettie—maiden name, Moore—was about the size of a full-grown rattlesnake: four and a half feet of pure venom. She weighed about eighty pounds, and with her close cap of dry red hair she looked like an oversize doll—if, that is to say, the doll had a frown molded on its face. One passion entirely possessed her: malice. She had never been heard to say a kind or even an indifferent word about anybody. Later on I came to despise her for it and to laugh at her, but when I was still too young to dare despise or laugh at my grandmother, the viciousness with which she attacked every person as

soon as he or she was out of hearing frightened and sick-
ened me. If she was right, then everybody was horrible;
if she was wrong, then she was. It made her feel superior
to others to suggest that they were fools to believe in
anybody's reputation as a good husband. Beats his wife,
she would assert. Worst skirtchaser in seven counties.
When it was objected that this was the very last man
of whom such things could be true, she would smirk
and say no more. If you enjoy being a fool, her smirk
said, pray, don't let me disturb you. What disappoint-
ments or what injuries had so stunted the growth of her
heart, which was dwarfed even out of proportion to the
rest of her, I do not know. It was impossible to imagine
a time early and innocent enough in her life when she
was anything but what I knew her—as it would be to
imagine a time in an alligator's life when it had an
agreeable disposition. My father could remember no
such time. It was sour milk that his mother had suckled
him on.

Will Humphrey was not much taller than his wife,
and a person who did not know him well might have
judged him to be not much less vicious. Will Humphrey
had not a drop of malice in him; he assented to whatever his wife said so as to keep peace between them. As
much as possible he kept out of reach of her tongue.
This was much, the length of her tongue notwithstand-
ing. His work kept him in the fields from dark to dark
nine months of the year. The rest of the time he spent
mending something or other, sitting in the sunshine or
out of the rain in the doorway of the barn. It would be
pleasant to be able to record that I felt drawn to my
grandfather in his loneliness, sorry for his poverty and
for the sourness of the atmosphere my grandmother

created for him. I did feel sorry for him, but I was not
drawn to him. He was so dispirited a man, so old-seem-
ing, so beaten down by life, that he was unapproachable.
According to my father, he was like that when he was
young, too. Even his music seemed to bring him no joy.
His face as he fiddled his wild hoedowns remained as
impassive as ever. And he played only for pay, never
for pleasure—his own or his family's.

He was, it was plain to see, part Indian. Which
meant that his father, long dead, had been even more
of one. This monosyllabic grandfather of mine, stolid
as an Indian, would, or could, satisfy none of my eager
curiosity about my Indian great-grandfather. With his
own son, when he was a little boy, inquisitive about himself and his origins, he had been just as uncommunica-
tive, and so I could learn nothing about us from my
father either. The Indian's squaw, my great-grand-
mother, also long dead, was said to have been a Gipsy,
and a fortune-telling one to boot. Once a man came to
her for occult guidance in finding a gold ring he had lost.
"It's underneath the pig trough," she was said to have
said, "where you put it to test me." She was right, of
course. That one anecdote was my total trove on her,
and it was more than I had on that brave, her husband.
I could spin romances around his name: Star Humphrey
—that was all. Is it that there is a sameness in hard, bare
lives, generation after generation, that makes them no
different from one another than two generations of oaks,
of animals? Or does the brutishness of such lives grind
down the memory, the curiosity, along with the body?
Illiterates make the best storytellers, it is said, and the
stories they tell are of the tribe. Not my forebears, who
for all the memory they had left, all that my father was

able to transmit to me, had done nothing but get born, breed and die.

Meals at the table in my father's boyhood home were short, and after the grace said mechanically over them, eaten in the silence of animals at their stalls. Prepared and served as a duty, the food was eaten as a necessity; no refreshment for the spirit was in it. The family's time together away from work made work seem a relief. The days were spent in mindless drudgery that gave them nothing to say to one another after supper in the evening. There was nothing to read, no urge to read anything, barely the ability. There was a musician in the family, but no mood for music. The nearest neighbors were miles away. The shortness of the answers they got to their questions about things dried up the boys' curiosity. There was nothing to do but go to bed. Most evenings they were too tired to do anything else anyway. Such news of the world as reached them was of lives as monotonous as their own. After a few years of that life, about the only use for his tongue that a person had was to curse.

Of this poor, loveless, drudging, mean-spirited household, dominated by that concentrated little dose of poison —Net, as she was called—where what little talk there was was her backbiting and stale scandal-mongering, the boy now became a full-time working member—and he began at once to dream and to scheme of a way out of it.

That spring he plowed and planted, that summer he chopped the cotton and hilled the corn, that fall he picked his own weight in cotton daily. Too short to husk corn, he shucked the ears and shelled them. He dug potatoes. He led the mule harnessed to the sweep in miles of circles around the mill as the sorghum cane was crushed.

And he saw half the syrup—the only sweetening he knew —go to the owner of the land on which the cane had been grown. He saw half the money for the cash crop, the cotton, too, go to the owner, and, in Lone Star, on the way home from Clarksville and the gin, saw the other half go to the owner of the crossroads store in settlement of last year's bill.

On that trip to Clarksville the boy saw his fate but did not recognize it. His first car. It was one of the first that Clarksville itself had seen—a thing as rare, and apt to remain so, as a chariot of the gods, dropped from the clouds. The boy had gawked at the curiosity along with the crowd, and then, seated on the tailgate of the wagon returning to the farm and the drabness of real life, had forgotten it long before they reached Lone Star. It was a thing remote from everybody's life, worlds removed from his. To the ten-year-old boy that first one gave no sign that its countless spawn would both deliver him and destroy him.

HE RAN AWAY FROM HOME that fall after the crops were in—he had stuck it out until they were. The work was actually lighter now, and there was some rest for his overworked little body but no relief; it was the same dreary season always in that house.

His mother knew where to find him. So did his father, but he dared not be the first to say it. In that house that he loved more than any other on earth and always would, for as long as he lived. It was to his Aunt Suzie, his father's sister, his only aunt, that he went as though home to his true mother. No matter where he and his family were staying, he always knew which way Aunt

Suzie's house lay, as a Mohammedan knows in which direction to pray. In later life, it was there he would go to visit his relatives, not to his parents, not until shamed into it by his wife (who enjoyed them as little as he did, but whose sense of filial duty was strong enough for two), taking me, who loved Aunt Suzie as he did.

That her son preferred his aunt to his own mother did not further endear Susan Sample to Nettie Humphrey, but she, who loved nobody, was the only person of all who knew Suzie who did not love her.

My Aunt Suzie was all the lessons anyone would ever need in the deceptiveness of appearances. Were I to have to choose one word to describe her, I would say she looked like a witch. She was skinny and bony, flat-chested as a plank. Her face was pinched, narrow, sharp, wrinkled. She had a long, pointed nose and a long, pointed chin, hollow cheeks with high, prominent cheekbones, reddened and roughened by exposure and by scrubbing with harsh lye soap. Hers was a face that spent no time before a mirror. But that uninviting-looking bosom was available for any troubled head to lay itself upon. Inside it beat a heart quick with concern and comfort. A disposition so agreeable lay behind those homely features that they themselves became identified with it. You would not have changed them if you could.

Hers was the spirit which set the tone of the house: busy, serene, cheerful, hospitable. Her husband, Uncle Joe, was a presence felt but seldom heard from. As silent a man as his brother-in-law, Will Humphrey, he gave an altogether different impression. His silence came from contentment. He was like a mule—born mute, but born strong, independent, self-sufficient, imperturbable. He participated little in the liveliness of his household, but he looked on with satisfaction. It was his wife's house (in my time, whenever a visit there was proposed—as it was at every possible opportunity—it was always, "Let's go to Aunt Suzie's!"). It was not that she was domineering; she was anything but that. And for her husband she had the greatest respect, for his uprightness, his gentleness as a husband and a father. It was that the house was her domain, as the fields were his.

Day began at the Samples' even earlier than at the Humphreys', and with even more chores to be done, but they were done in a different spirit, all hands willing and cooperative, which made the coming of day welcome, made the children clamber eagerly out of Aunt Suzie's mountainous feather beds. They were never up before she was. Aunt Suzie rejoiced in her daily duties. She had much to rejoice over.

First she milked and fed her seven cows, turned them out, and brought the milk to the spring-house. While she did this the children split kindling, brought wood to the range, water from the well. Jim—already as quiet as his father, sober, steady, dependable. Maxie, his opposite—gabby, giddy, irresistible. Bird—made of the same stuff as her mother, and cast in the same mold. Little Hubert—yet to show his colors: a toy for them all to play with.

The cows milked, Aunt Suzie cooked breakfast, a big, old-fashioned farmhouse breakfast with hot biscuits, fried ham, bacon and sausage meat, oatmeal, grits, gravy, for her family of six and whatever guests had spent the night. Breakfast finished and the table cleared, she washed the dishes—this without running water— and dried them and set the table for dinner. While the oven was still hot, she baked three skillets of cornbread to be crumbled and scattered to the chickens and to her turkeys—whose hidden eggs she was so keen at finding. Then she went to the spring-house, separated the cream and churned and molded the butter. Her eggs, butter and cream, the whey from the butter-making which she fed her pigs, were an important part of the family's income. After the beds were made, the house swept, mopped and dusted, she cooked dinner. This was the big meal of the day: more biscuits, meat which she herself had dressed or plucked, three or four vegetables, pie and cake, two at least of each. In the afternoon, unless this was a washday, she found time to work in her vegetable garden or among her flowerbeds. Supper, more dishes, then she was free to join the family in the parlor, telling stories, singing songs, though she occupied herself with sewing—"A person might as well be doing something with herself," as she said. There was never a waking moment when her hands were idle. And, looking worn, wasted, frail, on all this she thrived. She was not frail, she was just spare, pared down to the essential.

The same few, simple elements of life as at home— an entirely different life made out of them: that was what the boy found at his Aunt Suzie's.

It was Uncle Joe who gave to the atmosphere of the house its piety. He was a most God-fearing man. Well he might be! His was the God of the Presbyterians, the flinty God of the flinty Scottish Presbyterians—your cold-bath, salt-porridge and haggis-eating Presbyterians. This sort of God: once, when their torments became more than they could bear, the sinners in Hell organized. At a set moment they would all raise their voices as one, and this cry would reach Heaven and move God and He would relent.

"Lord," they cried on cue, "we did na ken."

And He, leaning out of His balcony and looking down, said to them, "Nay, ye did na. But ye ken weel noo!"

Joe Sample, if he could have gotten God's ear, would have put in a word for them, though fully expecting his impertinence to cause him to be sent to join them.

He officiated four times daily, in saying grace before meals, and, at night, before the lamps were put out and everyone sent to bed, each with his own candle, reading to the family and whatever guests were in the house a chapter from the Bible. He opened the book at random. If it fell open at Deuteronomy, he read the laws of Kosher diet, the arrangement of the tabernacle. If at Kings, he read the chronicles of the bloody wars of succession. It was all holy, all uplifting, every sacred word of it.

Thus it was totally by accident that he read one night:

> *A virtuous woman who can find?*
> *For her price is far above rubies.*
> *The heart of her husband trusteth in her,*
> *And he shall have no lack of gain.*
> *She doeth him good and not evil*
> *All the days of her life.*
> *She seeketh wool and flax,*
> *And worketh willingly with her hands.*
> *She is like the merchant-ships;*
> *She bringeth her food from afar.*
> *She riseth also while it is yet night,*
> *And giveth meat to her household,*
> *And their task to her maidens.*

.   .   .   .

She spreadeth out her hand to the poor;
Yea, she reacheth forth her hands to the needy.

.   .   .   .

Strength and dignity are her clothing;
And she laugheth at the time to come.
She openeth her mouth with wisdom;
And the law of kindness is on her tongue.
She looketh well to the ways of her household,
And eateth not the bread of idleness.
Her children rise up, and call her blessed;
Her husband also, and he praiseth her, saying:
"Many daughters have done virtuously,
But thou excelleth them all."
Favor is deceitful, and beauty is vain:
But a woman that feareth the Lord, she shall be praised.

She was totally unconscious of the hush, far deeper
than the one which customarily attended the Bible reading, that fell upon the room, or that she was in any way
the cause of it. She was conscious only of her nephew's
tears—for he was there, had run off from home again—
of how those verses must sting him, poor child of a
house wanting in all these blessings which were every
child's birthright.

When his parents came to get him and take him
home, he would see them—or one of his cousins would
and warn him—coming down the road in the wagon,
and he would hide in the barn loft or out in the thicket
behind the house. He surrendered finally out of love
for Aunt Suzie—who would have been glad to keep him
with her always—knowing that his mother would take
out on her his preference for her, knowing that in her
goodness and simplicity she was defenseless against

such meanness as was concentrated in her diminutive sister-in-law.

So HE STRUCK OUT for the big world. He quickly reached the end of his tether, slunk back in defeat and defiance, and more determined than ever. Thereafter, every chance he got, he ran away again. A duckling in a hen's nest, not knowing what his natural element was, only that he was out of it, he was trying to fly the coop before he was fledged.

On his short legs and with his empty pockets, he never got far down the road before hunger, fatigue, loneliness, nightfall, fear—yes, even homesickness—overtook him. Then back he came "with his tail between his legs," or was brought back by some neighbor "like the whole pup." Except that a strayed pet would have been welcomed back with more joy and affection. Not that in the mood he came back in he was one to elicit much joy or affection. Then he really behaved with the surliness of a wild creature in a cage. An invincible antipathy, as between inimical species, was building up between him and them. For the edification of his brothers he was punished. Afterwards he punished the one who had enjoyed seeing him get his: his baby brother, whom it would be right to call his mother's favorite but that would imply that she liked him best, whereas the truth was, she liked him only. This earned the boy more punishment, more of the curses and scurrility which he had come to take pleasure in; for if he was the imp of Hell his mother called him, what did that make her, his dam?

His brother Roy, older than he by two years, was

as determined as he was to make his getaway, but Roy had the patience, the sense that Clarence lacked. Roy was biding his time until he could make his break and keep going until he was beyond recapture. "You're still too little," he said. "You've got to be able to support yourself. You've got to be able to keep going till you're far enough from home that nobody knows who you are— whose you are."

That was right—he knew it was; yet, though he knew beforehand that he would only be driven back again and have to take his licking, he was off again the next time their backs were turned, his very littleness already the goad to him that it was always to be; for as time passed and he stayed the same size, the longing and rebelliousness inside him grew more confined, pressurized, explosive. Not just a duck, but a wild duck— that was what they were trying to coop. Clipping his wings might keep him from flying far, but not from attempting flight.

His parents never asked the boy why he ran away. They knew why. A boy ran away from home because he was a bad boy. Lazy, ungrateful, because he wanted to go off and get into trouble. The way to make him a good boy, obedient, industrious, appreciative of what was done for him, to make him want to stay home, was to take the hide off him with a harness strap and set him more chores to keep him busy. Waywardness was a weed that grew in the bed of idleness.

He agreed. I was always left confused by this whenever my father told me about his boyhood. Recounting it, he was resentful of his treatment by his parents; reflecting upon it, he agreed with them that he was a

bad boy and deserved all the beatings he was given—
and he saw no contradiction between these attitudes.
Beating him might not correct an incorrigible boy, but
you had to beat him. It was not that, having put his
childhood behind him and become a parent himself, he
was now standing up for parents as a lesson to me, his
child. He never put his childhood behind him; he more
than most men remained the boy he was, the bad boy,
contrary, unruly, lawless. I concluded that he thought
neither he nor his parents were right; all were wrong;
they were a pretty bad lot all around. That is what he
did think. And there was another contradiction. A
touchier man than he never lived, vain, cocky, one who
could not tolerate the least slight, and yet he held himself
and his family in low esteem. Perhaps that is not really
the contradiction it seems.

Whose you were: when he was a little older and
already a great deal tougher, when he had outgrown
childish fear, when he knew he had nobody to feel
lonely for, no home to feel homesick for, then the fugitive boy learned the full meaning of that phrase. A boy
was not his own, he belonged to his parents, they had
a right to his work, and grownups were all in league to
catch one another's runaway boys, return them home,
and put them to work again. It was not just *his* parents,
then, it was *parents* who were his enemies. And so he
learned, little, unloved, lonely creature that he was,
the solitariness, the slyness, the self-dependency, the
lawlessness of a wild animal, and he began to wear on
his face the expression that later never altogether left it:
watchful, wary, his penetrating black eyes (made all
the blacker by the lifelong paleness of his complexion)

never fully at rest. The man this boy would father
would look at life over the sights of a pistol.

WHEN THE CROPS WERE IN, the family feasted, glutted—
the one time of the year when they did. When there was
ice on the pail of water at the back door and on the cow-
tracks and on the trough in the barnlot for two or three
mornings running, and it looked as though the weather
would hold, then the family was up extra early next
morning and the chores were done even more quickly
than usual, one being omitted: slopping the hogs.

They would have gone all but meatless for months
now, and hunger and the scent of blood turned the boys
into little savages. While one drew at the well, the others
toted water to every available vessel. A fire was built
under the washpot. One of the boys shinnied up the tree
nearest the pigsty and hung a pulley from its limb. The
mule was harnessed and to the trace was attached a
rope with a singletree at its end.

The father finished whetting his knives, kept the
big one and gave the small one to one of the boys, rolled
up his sleeves, donned his apron—a towsack held up
with bailing wire—and took up his single-bit axe.

It never failed that the hogs, ordinarily so torpid and
so trustful, seemed now to comprehend these prepara-
tions, to sense their peril, and to dash around the sty
squealing with terror. Their fear helped harden the
boys' hearts against them.

Slops were sloshed into the trough, and hunger got
the better of the hogs' mistrust. While they fed, the
father stole up behind one of them. Over it he raised
his axe, blunt side down.

The instant the axe struck the animal between the eyes, the boy in charge of the mule lashed it with the reins, the boy with the knife leapt over the fence into the sty, and scarcely had the stunned hog sunk to its knees when its throat was slit, its hamstrings bared, its hind legs spread by the singletree. It was dragged to the tree, the rope disconnected from the trace, thrown to the boy perched on the limb, passed through the pulley, retied to the trace, the mule whipped up, and the hog hung upside down while blood still spurted from its gashed throat.

Buckets of boiling water were brought from the wash-pot and sloshed over the hog. Scalding whitened the rind. The bristles were scraped off with a drawknife, which nicked here and there, drawing thin red lines.

With his big knife the father laid the hog open with a single downward stroke from crotch to jaw. The air turned foul and the entrails came tumbling out, coiling together on the ground like a knot of worms.

The entrails were chopped into lengths, these drawn between the fingers to squeeze out their contents, and they were thrown into the washtubs full of water; they would make casings for the sausage meat. The body cavity, which steamed in the chill air, was propped open with a stick. More water, cold from the well, was brought and flung inside it. The ground was awash now, shoes muddy, bloody.

From the bottom up, which is to say, from the head down, the carcass was dismembered, the parts dealt with in the fashion proper to each. Into the meat grinder went the ears and the jowls; headcheese and the spicy forcemeat called "souse" would be made of these. The skull was split and the brains removed; these, scrambled with eggs, would make tomorrow's breakfast. The bacon slabs were cut away, carried to the smokehouse and hung on hooks from the rafters. The backbone and the spareribs: the family had been waiting all year for them —and would wait for another year before they again ate so much meat: these were to be eaten fresh, the ribs barbecued, the backbone braised in gravy, eaten with baked sweet potatoes. The shoulders and the hams would need much work: much rubbing in of salt and sugar— later; now salt them well and pack them in barrels and cover them in case the day warmed up and brought out flies. It was time to grind the sausage meat, time to empty the washpot, build up the fire, and render the lard. The cracklin's left in the pot would make cracklin' bread for a week. Scour the washpot by making lye soap from some of the lard. When the work was all done and the gory apron removed, the chitterlings stuffed with sausage meat, the hickory wood smoke curling from the flue of the smokehouse and the lard sealed in jars, and while the dogs licked the bloody ground, it was time to say once again that all of a pig was useful but the squeal.

THE COMING OF COLD WEATHER meant cutting and hauling wood. The wood you cut would not be the wood you hauled. The wood you hauled you would have cut the previous year, or the previous tenant would have. The wood you cut was for next year, for your use or for your successor's. It worked as it does when you build a fire at a public campsite: you use what the last fellow left for you, you gather some to leave for the next fellow. Except that in this case what you leave is enough to heat a house and cook for a family all year. And if you are tenant-farming, you cut a third over and above your needs, and this goes to the owner of the woodlot. The gasoline chain saw lies far in the future. You and your boys cut yours with a two-man crosscut saw, and you stoop low to cut it close to the ground; the owner wants no wood wasted, no tall stumps to have to pull out when this land comes to be cleared. You cut it in lengths and stack it in cords between two standing trees. The wood you take home you and your boys saw into stove-sized lengths with the bucksaw. These you split and stack out of the weather.

Left to cord the wood, the boy would sometimes hear the yapping of a feist terrier and from time to time the crack of a rifle or the rumble of a shotgun. Sometimes the hunter would come out of the woods into the clearing. The man would have had enough of hunting for the day but be unable to call his dog in. He would tell the boy the dog's name and say, "If he comes to your place, feed him and catch him and tie him up. I'll come get him next time I'm down here." While the man talked, the boy would steal glances at the gun he carried.

Seeking a hiding place, the runaway boy turned to the woods, and found there his natural element. Found it as surely as a duckling raised from the egg by a hen finds its way sooner or later to water. Had the world next door to his been watery, he would have longed to run away and go to sea; instead it was woods, woods almost as vast as the sea, and so he took to them. The woods were a place to hide. To hide from everybody. A place to explore. To be an idle boy instead of a boy forced to do the work of a man.

Now, when he could hold out no longer and was

driven home, after his beating came the catechism, the sermon.

Didn't he have any sense?

The answer to that—his own answer, sullen, defiant, to himself—was, no. Not if sense was what they had. No, and didn't want any.

Didn't he realize what he was doing? Didn't he know that you could get lost in there and never be seen nor heard tell of again?

So they said, but so far he had not succeeded in doing it. Next time. When he got a little bigger, could go in deeper, hold out longer. When he had himself a gun. Thus they with their warnings against them fixed the woods permanently for him as a refuge, a sanctuary, and for the rest of his life, when he and his wife were feuding, when his creditors were dunning him, the law hot on his trail, when his extramarital tangles got too complicated even for him, then he took to the woods, where nobody could find him. The start of his getting to be the one man who could find his way out of those woods, to whom the law itself would turn when a guide was needed, was as a boy trying his best to get lost in them. He became a hunter by beginning as the hunted.

All he ever needed to make him do a thing was to be told he must not. Boy and man, for as long as he lived, there would always be somebody to warn him against doing something and thereby pique him into doing it. Posted land, game seasons, speed limits, prohibited liquor, other men's women: just put a *Do Not* sign on something and he had to do it. Not that he was fearless; on the contrary, fear was his drug, his addiction. He depended upon a daily dose of it as a diabetic depends upon his insulin. He was a gambler whose stake—about all he ever had, boy or man—was himself.

From his parents' warnings he got the notion that the woods were like a whirlpool: just venture inside and you were caught up and whirled inextricably round and around to the center. And, indeed, the pull they exerted upon him was like that. He listened attentively to their warnings, and what he felt was an irresistible pull.

Snakes: the woods were infested with them. Diamondbacks, timber rattlers, tiny coral snakes with venom so poisonous that their victims were dead before they touched earth, cottonmouth moccasins that struck without warning, without provocation, not in self-defense but out of sheer viciousness, hatred of humans.

There were cottonmouths in there as big as he was. Yet, big as it was, you never saw one until it was too late, so invisibly did it blend into its surroundings. Within moments of being bitten, the victim's leg or arm began to swell and discolor, and he to stagger, vomit, faint, suffocate. He was lucky if death came quickly. If not, the swelling spread over his whole body, the bitten limb erupted in running sores, turned gangrenous, rotted off. This could last for weeks, with the sufferer out of his mind and raving. There was no cure, no alleviation. Relatives had been known to shoot victims to put them out of their pain, and the law to look the other way.

Backing to get away from one of those moccasins— if you were lucky enough to see it before it struck—you could step right into the jaws of an alligator. Ten, twelve feet long they grew, with jaws that opened wide enough to gobble a boy whole, teeth that could splinter a railroad tie. A blow from one's tail could crack your skull as easily as breaking an egg, crush you like a snail.

The boy did not disbelieve these stories. But he noted that his parents scared themselves with them as much as they did him. A wall of fear surrounded the woods for them. That was what he was looking for, would brave Hell for: a place where they were afraid to follow him. So it was not to disprove their stories but to verify them, to see the dragons in their den, that he went back, went deeper, into the woods.

MY FATHER had never been bitten in Sulphur Bottom by anything worse than a mosquito, but that was not because worse things were not there—it was because he was he.

He never said that. He never had to. Not to men who knew the woods. He never said it to others, either— those brash enough to judge from his example that conquest of the woods was something any man could do. He had his own way of reviving, from time to time, their respect for Sulphur Bottom.

In my time, the Bottom remained much as it had been from the beginning. Clearing was confined to its edges. Within it towered virgin oaks. Rattan vines connected the trees in webs that looked as though they had been spun by spiders from the age of the mastodons. Cane grew rooftop-tall in brakes as dense as fur, impenetrable. Its guardian monsters had kept the place inviolate.

Now signs of change were appearing. The man most responsible for them was the one to whom they were least welcome. Game bags of the size he brought out of there emboldened others. Motor cars—kept running by him—got more men there more easily. To discourage these trespasses upon what he considered to be his private preserve, my father periodically shot and put on display at his shop a particularly big moccasin, propping open the mouth to show its fangs and its deathly white interior. Or—but for this he needed help.

Whenever my father needed help, in anything, he got it from Wylie West, his carbon copy. Wylie had no more sense than he had. Wylie would have walked through fire if my father had gone first—as he would have done on a dare.

Wylie worked for my father. He worked at my father's shop. However, he did not work for the shop, he worked for my father. To Mr. Barton, my father's partner, Wylie paid no mind.

Had he been asked what his feelings toward Wylie were, my father, if he had not said, "That's none of your business," would have said, "He's a good nigger." In fact, Wylie was the one man he liked, trusted and respected. But the code governing relations between the races forbade that he show this, or even altogether admit it to himself—although my father was just enough of a maverick, and enough of an outsider without all that much social standing to lose, to test the code to the breaking point. Thus he saw to it that other white men, his customers at the shop, treated Wylie with a difference which must have galled them, and to Wylie said that if any of them gave him any trouble outside the shop, to let him know. With himself, of course, he expected Wylie to know his place. Wylie had gained my mother's approval by never turning his back on her, or on any other white woman. He bowed himself away from her back door. He mistered me. We took such deference as our due. We never questioned that Wylie did, too. Just one thing bothered me: I liked Wylie to an unacceptable degree, beyond what was tolerated. I had heard the term "niggerlover" and the contempt and hatred with which it was spoken. I had to be on guard against letting my fondness for Wylie show. In town, that is— another reason for my love of the woods. There, with no one to see us, we could be more free and easy with one another.

Whenever my father got to feeling that too many other hunters were poaching on his preserve, it was Wylie he took with him—and, once, me—there to find and bring out something to put a little caution into them.

The time they took me with them it was early fall. We boated in. We were going in deep. Because alligators, although there is the occasional odd man-eater, mostly shun people widely. We took with us a live duck in a cage. It was one of the flock of wild mallards that my father kept penned in our back yard for use as decoys.

A boat seemed hardly to be wanted on that water. It was so thick, so motionless with mud, it looked as though it could more easily be walked upon. The river led straight through the woods like an aisle, and down it we passed as silently as barefoot believers, our shoes left outside on the temple porch. When we had paddled a short distance, it was as though a door had closed behind us, shutting out the sounds of the world: a door as heavy as a temple's, a silence in which to have spoken would have been an irreverence. Yet it was not an empty but a populous silence, an attentive, even an inquisitive silence, one sensed. I felt myself to be an explorer, a discoverer. To have been met around a bend by a band of unknown Indians, holdouts in this, their last fastness, would not have astonished me.

The stillness, the sea-calm silence: that was the thing that struck me first about the deep woods, and which as it steadily deepened, steadily challenged and put in doubt my sense of myself, of everything. Timelessness hung like a vacuum over that vast, unvisited domain. For me, time was associated with sound, inseparable from it: the chatter and bustle of human affairs, the dependable chiming of my town clock, which I had heard within, at most, an hour after coming into the world, and with the comforting conviction that others were regulating their lives in synchrony with mine. Time was people, social life, the sharing with others of measured portions of the day, at school, at work, at play. Time was schedules to meet, anniversaries, celebrations, communions. This journey into silence was a journey into timelessness. And since time was commitments, responsibilities, I understood as never before the lure of these timeless woods for that half-wild father of mine.

We were wet from getting into the water to lift the boat over fallen logs that stretched from bank to bank. In places the river parted the cane that grew as thick as hair down to the water's edge. At our approach, herons white as linen napkins and folded together in pleats unfolded themselves and rose stiffly into flight. A flock of buzzards hung high overhead, moving with us as though we had them on strings, like kites. The trees grew in height as we penetrated deeper into the woods, giving the sense that we were descending an ever-deepening and darkening canyon. Wherever a limb overhung the water we stopped and inspected it carefully before passing under it. More than once we found what we feared: a moccasin stretched along it. The thing would gape at us, baring its fangs, the unearthly whiteness of its mouth, then slide leisurely from the limb and drop to the water like a large, ripe, poison fruit. As big around as a man's calf, some of them were.

We lunched in the boat on cheese, canned sardines, devilled ham, beans, chocolate bars—the provisions of boys playing hookey from school—then paddled on.

It was fun to frighten oneself with the thought that a volley of arrows might come any minute from out of the bushes along the banks. Much more real was the sense of being the first of one's kind ever seen here— such a curiosity as to stop the birds in their flight, the animals on their rounds. We had left behind all that made us familiar to ourselves. Although I was older and bigger now than ever before, the vastness and the changeless antiquity of the place made me feel very small and very, very young.

We pitched camp early enough to kill our supper. I was of an age now to be allowed to go off hunting on my own—of an age to know when I had reached the end of my tether, which was, within call of my father's hunting horn. This was an old steer's horn, gnawed by mice. When it was time to call me in, my father put it to the right-hand corner of his mouth, compressed his lips, puffed his cheeks, and out came a sound that carried in the stillness of the woods like a ship's horn in a fog. To me it was as welcome as its mother's call to a strayed calf. He sounded it at intervals until I found my way to him.

We divided the camp chores among us. Wylie set

the trotline, my father skinned the squirrels, I gathered wood. Together we peeled the potatoes and onions, scraped the carrots. While the stew simmered over the fire, the men drank whiskey. Night brought the woods to life with sounds. It was after dark that time was measured here: in the regular hooting of the owl. In bed after supper I felt my father reach over me and touch Wylie. I too had heard what he had heard; now I understood what it was. The distant bellow of a bull alligator, like some dinosaurian yawn in the night.

The men woke in the morning gray-faced with whiskers. This made them look even more ghostly as we all went about our chores in the gray light that filtered down to us from the narrow opening between the trees high overhead. Breakfast was fried catfish taken from the trotline, sweet black coffee. We broke camp and were on the water by sunup.

Now every twist in the river carried us farther from all we knew and were. No likelihood of being met by Indians here, hostile or friendly. Even the cries of the birds and the animals that occasionally broke the silence were strange—surely they came from creatures different from the ones in the alphabet book. And yet along with the sense of deepening strangeness came a sense of familiarity, as though one had been here before, but in another life. Then the cries of the animals seemed parts of speech, the language that had been spoken in that other existence, and we were led on by the feeling that soon, perhaps around one more turn, that long-forgotten, universal mother tongue would all come back to us. Here, untended since our expulsion from it, was surely the Garden that once was ours, where we had given the creatures their names. A little farther on, those names would recur to us, and they would all come meekly in answer to our call.

Late that second afternoon we found the sign we were looking for. Holes—big holes—dug into the river-bank. We made camp, but not nearby our find.

Come meekly in answer to his name—the beast I heard that night? Vast as the woods were, they were filled by the bellows that began when darkness was deep. It was as if the thing wished to be heard in the outside world—and as if it had a mouth adequate to the wish. Listening to it, lying close beside my father and feeling his intentness, I sensed in him regions as vast, as wild, as unknown to me as the wilderness we had come through to get to this spot. Other men, from time im-memorial, had cautiously avoided this place; what drew him in here to disturb the thing that made that dreadful noise? It was a sound both hideous and oddly pitiful— like the groan of some monstrosity, some horrendous mistake of nature, a creature of the darkest night, afraid to catch sight of itself or even of its misshapen shadow by day, raging against its own unbearable brutishness and the intolerable isolation to which it had been con-signed.

We returned to the spot on the riverbank early next morning. Now we carried with us two long poles, two saplings that the men had felled and trimmed and pointed at one end. They put me on the bank opposite from and a short distance upstream of the holes, then rowed themselves across. They took off their clothes and put them in the boat, keeping on their tennis shoes.

When they were stripped to the skin it was as though the two men had been picked to illustrate a lecture on the difference between the races, to show nature's vast variety. Wylie was as black as my father was white, and each extreme accentuated the other. Both were an absence of color, and seemed to have been cut out from the surroundings, leaving their outlines. Rather broad outlines they were. No longer the slender young man who married my mother, my father now weighed around 160. Wylie was somewhere near the same. Two short, thick-set, muscular little men—big men in miniature.

They loaded their .30-30 carbines, feeding the first cartridge into the chamber, seven more into the magazine. The loaded rifles were stood against trees at a distance from each other. The poles were planted in the bank.

The duck was taken from its cage and launched, and, as decoy ducks always did, tried to fly. Paddling rapidly to get up speed for the take-off and beating the water with its clipped wings, it succeeded only in churning up a commotion. Suddenly it sank. It did not turn tail up and dive as ducks do; it sank. One moment it was there, then, quicker than it could quack, it was gone. At that same moment there was a loud splash, or rather, two, and gone from the bank were the men.

They were under for a long time. First to surface was Wylie. A moment passed. Then for a second the surface swelled, as I had seen it do when a creek is dynamited: that instant after the detonation and before the eruption. Then out of the water and high into the air burst my father, hanging on to something long and live and in a convulsion of rage.

He had hold of an alligator fully nine feet long by its short forelegs, as one might pin a man's arms behind him. Wylie threw himself in their direction, and in the split second that the furiously lashing tail was away from him, lunged and grabbed the hind legs. The animal writhed, twisted, heaved. Firemen trying to hold on to the biggest and most powerful waterhose were never more flung about, for the animal's power exceeded that, and it had a will behind it and a brain, always brutish, always hostile, now enraged. There was no letting go; they were joined to the thing; both had to hold on— hold on truly for dear life. Having recovered breath, both were laughing, between grunts, as though they were having the time of their lives.

They wrestled that bundle of fury to the bank and heaved it out of the water. Sure as a cat, it landed on its feet, and like a cat it arched itself for battle. No step either toward the water or the woods did it take. It stood its ground.

It looked antediluvian, the one creature too totally malevolent to be taken aboard the ark, a monster from out of the primeval slime, gratefully thought long extinct. For a moment, until it moved, it looked clumsy. Not confounded—anything but; alert throughout its length; but out of its element, ponderous, ill-equipped for dry land. Not so; it was highly adaptable. It circled now, seeking its enemy, and its motions were as sure as though it moved on treads—truly amphibious: an all-purpose engine of destruction, designed to be invulnerable. Armor-plated with a scaly hide as hard as horn and triply armed it was, formidable from every approach, with its powerful long tail, the claws of its huge, half-webbed feet, the terrible teeth of its enormous chops bared permanently in a zestfully malicious, a murderous grin. Its forelegs folded like elbows, its hind legs like knees; it stood like a man lying on his stomach about to do a push-up. Now it straightened and stiffened its legs, erecting itself to its full fighting height. It hissed as loud as a steam locomotive and the spray of muddy water from its nostrils made it appear to be snorting smoke. The grating together of the scales of its tail as it lashed from side to side made a swish in the air like a volley of bullets. It stood its ground, ready and a match for anything that lived, superb in its fearsomeness.

Its only moment of irresolution came when the two men clambered onto the bank and it had to choose which one to go for first. It went for Wylie. And its gaping jaws made it appear to be guffawing at the puniness of its opponent. Wylie had plucked his pole out of the ground and now he jabbed the creature with it as it stalked him. Undeterred, it attacked, bellowing, hissing, its tail lashing steadily to ward off the enemy at its back, all the while making that metallic, multi-scaled sound like the rustle of a coat of mail. As it forced Wylie back and back I expected to see my father go for his rifle, but he was enjoying the sport and instead he gave the creature a whack on its tail and a bellow in imitation of its own. It answered with a bellow, swivelled around and advanced, hissing hideously, on him, its tail keeping that wide swath cleared behind it. Now my father jousted with it while Wylie harried it with whoops and hollers.

Like a pair of matadors they teased it by turns, working it into a fit of fury. It seemed to grow, to swell with the mounting pressure of its frustration and to become still more menacing and terrible. Quicker, too.

It made a dash at my father. He thrust at it with his pole. Flinching, it retreated, then before my father could ready another thrust, it had his pole, snapped it with a bite, and as it came on toward him seemed to be grinning for the kill. In dashed Wylie from behind. But it was intent now upon its disarmed enemy and not to be distracted by the blows, thick and heavy as they were, on its back. They sounded as though they were falling on something as solid and insensitive as a turtle's shell.

My father was running backwards but the animal was fast closing the gap that divided them, its jaws gaping wide, when Wylie found a vulnerable spot. Where the hind leg joined the body his spear drew blood. Blood, and with it, the loudest bellow yet. The animal turned on him. My father turned too and sprinted for his rifle.

Goaded into a frenzy of hate and frustration, the animal propelled itself at Wylie, who dropped his spear, turned and ran for his own rifle. He had not yet reached it when my father, with his, leaped over that constantly lashing tail and came down astride the animal, firing even before he touched the ground. Though it stopped, the animal gaped hugely, reared so high on its talons that it looked as though my father was riding on its back and it was trying to throw him, then gave its tail a lash that seemed meant to demolish all the world behind it. Then its legs folded and it sank upon itself, its weight forcing its jaws shut.

As the two men, like naked savages, did their victory dance around it, whooping and yelling and pounding each other's backs, the alligator's tail died segment by segment, down to the tip. When that final bit stopped twitching and death distended the animal, it flattened and widened on the ground, its relaxation causing its teeth to grate for one last time.

Afterwards, when I asked my father whether he had not been scared, he said yes, very. I disbelieved that of my father, but I was grateful to him for saying it.

It took some of the taint of childishness off the fear I had felt.

Placed on exhibit at the garage with its jaws propped open, that dragon was more effective than signs posted all around Sulphur Bottom saying, "Danger. Keep Out. C. Humphrey, Prop."

So WHEN THE OUTLAW, the killer—or would-be killer (the filling station attendant whom he had shot was still alive)—took to the woods, it was to my father that County Sheriff Ross Smiley came for help.

The two were old friends. The Sheriff had more than once chased my father and let him get away as he brought a carload of liquor over the line from neighboring, wet Lamar County into ours, which by local option was dry. The times were hard and a little extra money was to be picked up by moonlighting at this, though the competition was keen and others in the same racket were not above giving the Sheriff a tip-off whenever a competitor was known to be making a haul. The Sheriff was not himself much of a booster for the Volstead Act, and he suffered when, to destroy the evidence, the bootlegger he was after smashed a case of good whiskey on the highway; but the local Baptists had to be pacified this way every now and again, especially around election time, for, as was always said—and still is—Red River County drank wet but voted dry. The Sheriff and his wife had been our guests one hot evening in the house on Third Street when an intermittent series of noises like muffled firecrackers was heard from somewhere inside the house. We knew what it was and we pretended not to have heard anything. It was my father's bottled homebrew popping off its caps in the heat, and, as we also knew, spraying the clothes in the closet on the floor of which it was stored. It was the Sheriff who finally said, "For God's sake, 'Ump, don't just sit there, attend to that beer before it's all gone! And if you've got any on ice, for God's sake, let's have some! I'm as thirsty as a mop."

The holdup and shooting was two days old and the fugitive, who had taken to a back road to evade the roadblocks thrown up for him, had run out of gas and abandoned his stolen car and taken to Sulphur Bottom, had been in there since the previous afternoon, when the Sheriff came to my father with a request that he guide a posse in pursuit of him.

"Nuh-uh. Not me," was my father's answer.

Next day the Sheriff was back to appeal to him again. He said his wife would never permit it. To the Sheriff's assurances that no harm would come to him, that he and his men would be there to protect him, his reply was, "If I was to tell Ross Houston that, he would cancel my insurance policy. You nor none of them deputies of yours could hit a bull in the ass with a paddle. I'd feel safer with this boy of mine along. He's a better shot than any you've got. Ain't you, littl'un?"

In the meantime, however, his imagination was at work. While the Sheriff was appealing to his civic sense, of which he had none whatever, he was projecting himself into the feelings of the fugitive, a class with which he felt a natural affinity, and sympathizing with anybody who had strayed into those woods without knowing them as he, and only he, did. So on the next day he gave in and agreed to go—not to capture the man, but to rescue him.

When my father found the gunman—and that was

not until noon of the second day of his search—he had been in there going on five days. Still he was not ready to come out peacefully.

My father did not try to keep the man from knowing he was being trailed. Nor did he try to create the false impression that he himself was any more than a lone man. He wanted him to think that he was being closely stalked; he wanted him not to think that he was out-numbered, not to think that he was about to be ambushed, not to panic. To the Sheriff's question, how many men did he want to accompany him, he had answered, "None. I don't want to have to keep track of them, too. I don't want a lot of guys threshing around and raising a ruckus. I don't want them getting our man edgy, or getting jumpy themselves and going off half-cocked. I don't want no part of any shoot-out. Either I go all by myself or else I won't go."

"Have it your way. I'll deputize you."

"Oh, no, you won't. I expect that fellow's not too fond of sheriffs or sheriffs' deputies. Thanks all the same."

"You can't arrest him without authority."

"I don't intend to arrest him. I just intend to bring him out. You can do the arresting."

"Take my pistol."

"No, thanks. I told you I don't want no part of any gunplay. I don't want any trouble with this fellow. I want him to be glad to see me."

But he was not. Not yet. Not even after going on five days in there. He was still dangerous, still unapproachable, trapped but untamed. Weary, hungry no doubt, thirsty no doubt, lost—but still with fight in him, still quick to bare his fangs, that is to say, to reach for his pistol, as my father ascertained by testing him with a noise, still ready to make his stand and shoot it out rather than be brought in.

So my father let him know he was in the vicinity, as if to say, "Whenever you're ready, here I am," and he quit eating the food and drinking the water he had brought. This might take longer than he had reckoned on, and these he would need as barter, as bait.

Meanwhile it was not just a waiting game he played with the man throughout the rest of that day, the next, and into the next. He guided him as if he had reins on him and a pair of blinders like those on a plowhorse, so that it can see only directly ahead of it down the row you wish it to follow, not to its sides. He drove him hard and fast and without rest. He kept him constantly on the move, and whenever he took a turn which my father knew might in time lead him out to a road or to one of the farmhouses in the clearings around the margins of the woods, he yanked the opposite rein, that is to say, he closed in on him and turned him the way he wanted him to go.

From his footprints my father deduced that the man was a town man. At least, he was not shod appropriately for the place he now found himself in. Those pointy-toed oxfords were for paved streets. So at night he serenaded him with all the sounds calculated to keep a city man lost in the woods awake, even one without the law in pursuit of him. He keened like a screech owl. He barked like a fox. He bellowed like an alligator. He squalled like a bobcat. And although they were long extinct in Sulphur Bottom, and, as he said, he himself had never heard one outside of a picture-show, he howled like a lone wolf in the night.

He still had not seen his quarry. It was now as though he had a big fish on the line, waiting for it to tire and break water, show itself to him. Meanwhile he knew by ear exactly how far from him he was at all times, as surely as a fisherman knows from the quantity of line on his reel how deep his fish has sounded. Gradually he closed in, as a fisherman reels in and gains line on a stubborn but tiring fish. By noon of the third day he was ready for the net.

An order to him from out of hiding to throw his pistol as far from him as he could and strip was then all that was needed. After he was dressed again, fed and watered, he was brought out and turned over to the waiting Sheriff. Judging him now to be near collapse and not wanting to have to carry him, my father had been steering him out all that morning. When he surrendered they were within a quarter of a mile of the road.

OUT OF THE WOODS came the first money the boy ever earned. In the barn on one of the places they stayed on he found a few rusty old steel traps. These he baited and set in the sloughs and the bayous. He trapped muskrats, coons, an occasional red or gray fox. He ran his line in the morning before beginning his day's work. Lacking a gun, he carried a club to kill the animals with.

He made stretchers for his skins, sawing them from a plank and rounding one end and smoothing the edges with a piece of bottle glass. The skins were removed whole, like a pullover sweater, stretched over the boards and the flesh and the fat scraped off. When they were fleshed they were salted; when dried stiff, removed from the boards. He sold his skins to the keeper of the cross-roads store at Lone Star.

To the store at that season of the year came a special class of men—or men whom the season lifted out of their class and into a special one. Not there now for the dull business of trading, these men were hunters. The contrast between them and his own plodding, pleasure-less father shamed the boy. Some of these men were sharecroppers themselves, but they had in them a spark that his father lacked—that spark of response to a world beyond grubbing and hoeing in the dirt, a quality that took them out of themselves and into something bigger, older and longer-lasting than themselves. Each pursuing the most solitary of pastimes, there was yet a feeling of fraternity among them. Their dogs were hunting dogs, not dooryard mutts, with blood-lines like nobility, bred and trained, with that look of the pampered and idle, the sporting class. Some of them had reputa-tions countywide. Leaning against the wall of the store would be the hunters' guns. The boy dared not look at them as long as he would have liked. If no hunter ap-peared while he and his father were there, he could gaze at the two or three old muzzleloaders that the store-keeper had for sale, battered veterans with the stocks splintered at the grip, held together with wire—even these hopelessly beyond his dream of owning. He gave serious thought to stealing one, was deterred by his certainty that his longing for one, which he supposed must emanate from him like musk, would point the finger of suspicion directly at him.

The little money he got for the sale of his skins kept

alive his dream of one day owning a gun. A gun would free him, make him independent, self-reliant, and would arm him to resist recapture. With a gun he could run away from home and never be brought back. Goodbye to chores, to chopping and picking cotton, cutting wood. He would live like an Indian—which in part he was— live in and off the woods. He would make himself clothes from the skins of animals, shoes from their hides. What he required that the woods could not provide, he would steal, like the Indians, like the animals themselves. He would come out of the woods at night as the coons and foxes did and raid his father's cornpatch, his mother's kitchen garden. When he got to wanting a chicken he would steal one from the chickenhouse. And for his one essential, ammunition for his gun, he would trade—trap and trade skins.

Sitting on the gallery of the store or inside around the stove, the hunters complained of the scarcity of game. They remembered when they were able in half a day, in a half-mile walk, to fill a buckboard.

No wonder the boy had to go in deep to find them. What did they expect? For the animals never to learn, to adapt, to keep on coming back generation after generation to the slaughter? To keep coming back to woods that were thinned further each year, where there was less for them to feed on, less cover to hide in, more hunters than ever out to kill them?

"Go in there deep enough," someone always said, "and you'll still find them."

And someone else: "Yeah, but who's going to find you?"

The boy listened, solemn-faced, wide-eyed, unnoticed, and kept his silence. It was not for one his age to claim to know more than grown men knew. Besides, he was not aware of what he knew. By then he knew things about the woods that he did not know he knew, and certainly not that he was the only one who knew.

And so he was as surprised as the men, and possibly as skeptical, when the storekeeper said, "That boy there. Him there" (for it was possible in a sweep of the eyes to miss him)—"he can take you anywhere you want to go in there. What's more, he can bring you out again."

He looked hardly big enough to know his way home. But maybe if you did not take him far enough to tire out his short legs, so that you wound up having to carry him out on your back, he could make himself useful, in the absence of a dog, as your turner. You required a turner, hunting squirrels: a boy or a noisy dog to go around to the other side of the tree and keep the squirrel from turning as you turned and keeping the trunk between you, as one would do by the hour if the tree was an isolated one and it could not leap to another.

So he began to go into the woods with them, and hunters coming back with game bags fuller than they had been in years said to the storekeeper, "That boy is a cutter!" Then men he never saw before, from Clarksville, Bogata, Detroit, Fullbright, would ask for him, that little button-eyed, cottonheaded tyke that could take you in there and put you on gamestands like you never saw before, and who could outlast you, was sorry to come in when you were ready to quit. His father even excused him from some work, because he took from the boy the dime or the two-bits he was tipped for his services. He was still as far from a gun as ever while craving one all the more, having had a taste of it, when he was sometimes allowed by a hunter to shoot his.

THE BOY'S FATHER was one of those row-crop farmers with no feeling but hostility for land not cleared, productive, profitable. He longed for a piece of farmland of his own so much, and so hopelessly, that he resented that worthless woodland of which a wilderness surrounded him. From such a father, a boy longing for a gun could hope for no sympathy, not even if he had had the money to give him for one. Too poor to buy a gun, even to hope to buy one so long as he was only a boy and not earning wages, son of a man who himself held cash money in his hand just once a year, the boy realized that there was only one way for him to satisfy his longing.

A breechloader, using factory-made shells, was beyond him. Boughten shells using smokeless powder were too powerful, required a gun made of proof steel, a firing chamber capable of withstanding great gas pressure, a moving block, a firing pin too complex for his tools, his skill. But in those days there were still in use a great many old percussion cap and ball muzzleloaders, and stores still stocked black powder, caps and bulk shot for them.

His father had tools and a forge, as did every farmer, for home blacksmithing jobs, and the boy, already mechanical, was always using them to make himself something or other. No notice was taken, no questions asked about what he was up to now. Questions from them about what he was up to usually got no response anyway.

He found a length of small-gauge iron pipe threaded

and capped at one end. Its thickness made it heavy and so he dressed it down with a file. Only a child or a life-term prisoner, a sailor or a lighthouse keeper would have had the patience. He filed a hammer and trigger out of a bar of scrap iron, shaped a lock and fitted it with a flat spring. Three stocks he had to carve, with grooves for the barrel and the ramrod, before he got one right. He forged two barrel bands from harness rings. From the hickory handle of a worn-out hoe he whittled a ramrod. He made himself a powderhorn. By then he had turned another year.

On his annual trip into Clarksville to the gin that fall he brought the metal parts with him, secreting them beneath the wagonbed. He took them to a machinist in town. He ordered the man to drill and tap a hole in the barrel and insert the threaded nipple for the caps, drill screw holes in the lock. Fingering in his pocket the dollar and a quarter that was his capital, he asked how much he owed. The man refused payment. He would repay that mechanic's favor to him many times over by making and repairing in his own shop anything he could that any boy in town asked him to.

It was the last of his many guns that he would really care for. He used a gun hard, took care only of its mechanism, not its looks, and when one was used up, got another one. So long as one came to his shoulder right, functioned mechanically, he cared little or nothing about its appearance. His were strange-looking things, built like he himself was built: sawed-off. Not at the muzzle, but at the butt. Standing, a gun of his looked as though it was resting in a hole. The reach of his arms was short; to accommodate it, he sawed about three inches off his gunstock. This made the gun muzzle-heavy, but the muzzle could not be shortened without removing the choke. To compensate, he drilled holes in the stock beneath the buttplate and filled them with lead. Once that was done to a gun, he was deadly with it.

The boy hid his finished muzzleloader in the rafters of the barn. Next time his father drove to the store he went along with a bundle of skins which he meant to trade, on the sly, for powder, caps and shot. He clambered up the wheel spokes, onto the hub and over the sideboard, and he saw lying on the wagonbed, beneath the seat, his gun. He took his place on the seat. As they were crossing the bridge over Scatter Creek, his father whoaed to the team. He reached under the seat, brought out the gun and flung it into the creek. Whereupon, from his side of the bridge, the boy flung his bundle of skins into the creek. His father flicked the reins and the team moved on.

My heart broke for the poor boy when my father told me this story. He laughed. "He" (meaning his father) "was right," he said. "I doubt" (trans: I do not doubt) "that thing would have blown up and killed me the first time I pulled the trigger."

MY FIRST SHOTGUN cost a nickel. One chance on the punchboard in a diner on the Paris road where my father stopped one day just when it was getting time his boy, about to turn twelve—which was to say, going on thirteen—had a shotgun and learned how to use it. It was a four-shot bolt-action .410—the smallest of all the gauges. Being the lightest to carry, the cheapest to shoot, and the one with the least kick, it was the gauge boys were apprenticed on. From that beginning the grades up were 20, 16 and 12. It ought to have been just the other way 'round. Throwing the smallest charge and carrying the least far, the .410 ought to have been the gun for the most refined wingshot—the one in a thousand who is born, not made.

Now instead of stationary targets I began shooting at moving ones, or rather, I followed with the gun waiting for them to stop moving and become stationary. Finally, before the bird flew out of range or the rabbit hopped out of sight, I fired, and watched it fly on, hop faster. "You're trying to aim. Don't. You've got to shoot at where it's going to be," my father told me. "If you shoot at it, then you've shot at where it just was." For my age I was a pretty good rifleman—and for a wingshot I was a pretty good rifleman. To my father it was being a wingshot that separated the men from the boys. He was the best of them all, and I, his only son, his sole hope for a successor, could not get the hang of it. My father was patient with me but I was impatient with myself.

During my twelfth summer I would meet my father at the garage at quitting time and we would drive out of town to the nearby farms where mourning doves flocked to feed on the sorghum and the durum and to the stock-ponds to drink. That was the summer I shared with my chum Pete Hinkle a passion for casting, painting and warring with lead soldiers, and after a day of this, Pete sometimes went with my father and me dove shooting. I was not embarrassed to have Pete see me miss time after time, for Pete was no better shot than I was, though with his gun, a 20-gauge double barrel, he ought to have been.

We crouched in the tall grass at the edge of the pond,

the telltale white of our faces shaded by long cap-bills. A whistle from my father signalled the approach of a bird: one if from the left, two from the right. He gave first chance at every bird that winged in to us, and Pete and I took turns missing them, sometimes missing the same one in turn, before my father brought it down. It ran head-on into the charge of shot waiting for it in the air, crumpled and fell. It was left to lie where it fell. When the day was over, Pete and I gathered them up like nuts from a thrashed tree, wading for those fallen into the pond, searching for the others among the grass, my father directing us to them, he having marked them down, and kept tally of the bag.

In the course of the summer both Pete and I unavoidably got a little better at it. I began to think that the knack was not hopelessly beyond me after Pete lent me his gun a few times. My improvement with the 20 gauge raised my self-confidence and I shot better with my own gun. I had learned what deceptive birds doves are. They looked slow and as if they ought to be easy to hit but they were fast and their flight erratic and unpredictable, capable of sudden acceleration, full of dips and flares, tricky as a pilot dodging flak. You swung from behind, passed it firing and followed through, stringing out the charge in a path on the air ahead of the bird. And you still missed a great many more than you hit.

MY PERFORMANCE ON DOVES qualified me to be taken quail shooting in the fall. For, although quail are actually easier to hit than doves, they occupy a higher niche in the hierarchy of game birds, possibly because of their comparative scarcity, possibly because they are more prized on the plate. Whatever the reason, the rule is immemorial and inviolable: doves are boys' game, quail men's.

But I could not hit them. On this superior bird, this man's game, and being privileged for the first time to shoot over dogs, I did less well than I had done on doves. The joy of shooting over field dogs had been impressed upon me but it was something that until now I had had to take on faith from my father, just as I took on faith (although about this I had reservations) that the time would come when I would enjoy doing what he had recently told me men did with women.

His bird dogs at that time—"ours," he now began calling them—were Mack and Kate, brother and sister English setters, he white speckled with black, she black spotted with white. Though still young, they were, in my father's opinion, already the best dogs he had ever owned. They were completing their training as I was commencing mine. We could look forward to years of pleasure out of them.

He was right about the joy of watching good bird dogs at work—maybe about that other business too, then. To see Mack and Kate divide a field between them in quarters and cover its every yard, their tails like flags for us to follow, watch one of them suddenly brake, stiffen, straighten its tail, and the other one then come to honor its set, to watch them inch up on the covey just enough to hold it, not enough to flush it, was as thrilling as my father had told me it was.

That was my job: to flush the covey, and it was one reason I could not hit the birds. They could never be seen until they broke, for they were the color of autumn, of nature: of dead leaves, dry grass, twigs, mottled rocks, sunshine and shadow, and, up to the last moment, they could hug the earth as though made of it. When I kicked and they burst at my feet it was as though I had stepped on a landmine. Like shell fragments they went whirring off in all directions. Their flight was low to the ground and short. You had to be steady, cool and quick, and I could never recover from my shock in time to get off a sensible shot before they had all pitched to the ground. To think of ever being able to drop one, then swing on a second, even a third, on a single rise, as my father did consistently, seemed as unlikely for me as did that other business. The long fall season reached closing day without my having cleanly killed a single bird. Some at which we had both fired my father credited to me, but he was just being fond.

By then—closing day—no longer was the burst at my feet when I kicked quite so explosive. The big coveys, disbanded by gunning, thinned by predators, were broken up into singles, doubles, triples now. Still, I was sluggish in my responses, and instead of pointing my gun, I pottered.

We had had the morning to hunt. Now it was almost noon and we were working our way back to the car, my father's game pockets, as always, bulging, mine, as always, empty, when, emerging from a woods into a clearing, the two dogs simultaneously set. Tails stiff and straight out behind them, heads high, they seemed to be holding the birds transfixed by their steady stare.

When I kicked, three birds flushed, two one way, one another. So rapid were my father's two shots that they seemed one, and to each a bird, in a burst of feathers, fell. I in my pottering way was following the lone bird, when my father swivelled, found it and fired.

He scored a clean miss. I fired, and in a third burst of feathers on the air, that bird fell.

I acted as though I was used to doing it daily. So did my father, and he was offhand in his congratulations to me. But he was almost visibly puffed with pride. That he himself had missed the bird doubled his pleasure.

Forgotten were the uncountable number of quail he had brought down in his time whenever he told the story of that one of mine. Before long he was omitting to mention the two he had gotten on that rise before I killed the one he had shot at and missed.

Counting my one, we took home fifty-three quail that day. Game was not a treat for us, it was the staple of our diet; butcher's meat was the rarity in our house. My girl-mother, until late in the night, plucking birds into a washtub and sneezing as the feathers or the down tickled her nose, is one of my most vivid images of her, as is the one of my father stepping on the tail of a squirrel and peeling it out of its skin. Despite my mother's thoroughness as a housekeeper, pinfeathers and wisps of fur floated around doorjambs and lingered in corners of our house. The habit of watching for birdshot in my meat was so ingrained in me that I sometimes forgot and did it while eating fried chicken.

Yet it would have surprised my father to be called a gamehog. He was simply providing for his family. To the question, "What if everybody killed as many as you do?" he would have answered, "But not everybody does" (refraining out of modesty from saying, "Nobody does"), and would have expected that answer to quiet the fears of anybody concerned (in those days few were) over the future of wildlife. He heard men complain about the scarcity of game, but he had been hearing that all his life, and always from the same ones: those who were not very good hunters. There were good years and bad years, as there had always been, as there were for any of nature's crops. The long recent drought had had an effect, but that was coming to an end now, and once the birds and the animals rebuilt their numbers, we would see good times again.

THAT ONE CLOSING-DAY QUAIL of mine earned me the right to be taken a time or two that winter to shoot over the water, at the game bird supreme: wild ducks. Only a time or two, for duck shooting is where not merely the boys but the lesser men are separated from the men. Not just because ducks are the hardest to hit of all moving targets, but also because duck shooting is done under conditions demanding uncommon patience, stamina and strength.

The use of live decoys in shooting ducks had been outlawed the previous year, or maybe the one before that; but my father was never a strict observer of any of the game laws. In this he was not alone among hunters in our parts—just the most flagrant violator. Game laws were unenforceable there in those times. No effort was even made to enforce them. The post of warden, if not vacant, was held by somebody I had never heard of. Somebody who wisely worked not very hard at the job. To have done so would have made a man highly unpopular there where men had always hunted for meat, and took it as their fundamental and inalienable right to go hunting whenever they felt like it and to be limited in their kill by nothing but their own prowess—and where judges and juries agreed with them wholeheartedly. Gentlemen-sportsmen are not found on the frontier; and although the frontier was gone, and my father was one of those responsible, men like him had yet to learn this. Federal game laws like those protecting migratory birds they thought were something applicable to the other states of the Union, perhaps, but not to Texas.

My father kept his flock of live decoys in our back yard—whenever we moved, they moved with us—and he still drove through the square with them quacking loudly in their cage affixed to the rear of the model T touring car he used for hunting, and which could get with equal ease through the mud of Sulphur Bottom or the sand spread thickly for miles by the Red River in its periodical risings. Mallards, his were: three dozen of them, the imbalance between the sexes favoring hens over drakes. Siren-songs they quacked to their former fellows.

The wildfowler loves foul weather. Then the birds are on the wing. When days are short they must be active during the few daylight feeding hours. Rain and fog hamper their vision. Fearing freezing of their feeding grounds, they are on the move. The gunner endures these conditions in order to take advantage of the pressures they put upon the birds. Always on my initiatory expeditions to the Red River, it had been raining, was raining, and was going to rain—cold, cutting rain, often mixed with sleet, with a steady north wind driving it.

Even the model T could get us only so near the water. From our stopping place we proceeded on foot —all thirty-eight of us.

My father had rigged a stout cord, like a trotline, to which, every few feet, instead of a fishhook, was attached a snap swivel. Each duck was banded on one leg, and like convicts in a chain gang marshalled out of their van and manacled and marched to their work on the road, they were snapped to this cord—we two their shotgunned guards. Leading the column was always the same bird, an old drake that had established himself as gang-boss.

When the decoys were on the water we took our places in the blind, my father wiping out behind us with a bough the footprints we left in the wet sand. The blind was a pit dug into the sandbar and slant-roofed with reeds. To see out, I stood on a crate.

Our watch of the gray skies would go long unrewarded. Then out of the mist they would suddenly appear like a squadron of fighter planes in formation streaking to intercept the enemy. Immune to the seductive quacking of our decoys, some, high out of range, swept on. But another flock would bank and turn, circle, circle again more narrowly, dip, dive, and then you could hear the whistle of their wings as they swooped low overhead. "Pintails," my father would whisper, or "Mallards." What he said that gave him the most satisfaction was "Canvasbacks!"

He considered that the new law limiting duck shooters to three shots, one in the firing chamber and two in the magazine, was also for those who chose to obey it. As he always had, he carried five in his hammerless pump 12 gauge with the long, full-choked barrel, and I was to see him drop five birds on one pass, beginning with the hindmost and working forward so the flock could not count its losses.

When hit, ducks did not fold up and tumble down.

Their speed seemed hardly to slow. They sailed on in a steadily falling trajectory and crashed into the water like a plane with its pilot dead at the controls.

The newly established daily limit on ducks was twenty-five. Since I was not able to fill mine myself, my father did it for me. That was only fair, as I was a beginner, and handicapped, undergunned. I tried my father's big gun and did no better with it than with the .410, getting nothing but a bruised shoulder in reward. I never minded. I was started now, in me my father was rediscovering the joys of just starting, and under his eager tutelage I was sure to show steady improvement.

ON MORNINGS WHEN MY FATHER TOOK ME HUNTING with him we would get to the woods at about the hour my mother and I had gotten to the Paris hospital in the ambulance with him that morning. But in the woods it would seem like the hour just before Creation. It was as if God said again each day, "Let there be light." Looking just as they must have on the first day, the woods took shape out of the void. The change seemed chemical, like a photographic print in the developer in the dimness of the darkroom, the image appearing out of nothingness, then rapidly becoming distinct, recognizable, familiar. The transformation in my father seemed chemical, too. Perhaps even more in recent years, when illness and disappointment and worry had borne him down, that old boyish wonder of his whenever he went to the woods made a boy of him again. In me he saw the boy he once had been and then for a time he was one again himself. My oneness with him gave me some of his sense of oneness with that world.

He and I had long ago dispensed with talk while hunting. I knew what was expected of me. If, for instance, we were there now, as soon as the woods were light I would have crept around to the other side of that oak, and that first squirrel that came out to feed and chatter would now be lying on the ground, brought down by that keen right eye that would never look down a gun barrel again.

IV

WORD OF OUR TROUBLES spread by phone, bringing our relatives—my mother's people—to join us in our vigil on the hospital grounds. I shied from them, from their attempts to comfort and to cheer me. I began to burrow into that mood which was to govern me for the next three days, and to culminate in my scandalous behavior.

I thought I detected something more than sorrow and concern for my mother and me in the looks on her people's faces. They seemed to share an understanding. They seemed to be saying to themselves—among themselves—"I always knew it would come to something like this one day."

I wanted to say to them, "I know what you're thinking. It isn't true! It isn't fair! Once upon a time, yes. But not any more. Not for years."

I remembered the dreadful summer—the one before last—in Hot Springs, Arkansas, where he had gone on the advice of yet another doctor to take the waters and the baths. Scalding water and steam baths for a bleeding peptic ulcer! The cafe in downtown Hot Springs where for twenty-five cents you ate all you could—delicious food!—and he, who loved to eat, loved spicy dishes, hot sauces, rich, indigestible sweets, fighting back tears as he studied his plate of mashed potatoes or dry white rice. Even worse, the six months following our return to Clarksville, when he had had to give up all solid food, when I was sent to his shop twice daily, at noon and after school, with a half-gallon of warm milk in a thermos. He waited until I was gone to drink it, ashamed to expose to his son this unmanliness which he had brought upon himself through his intemperance. His supper was the same, and so my mother and I ate ours early, in time to have the table cleared and the dishes washed and put away and the house aired to clear it of the smell of food.

"If you only knew!" I could have said to my mother's knowing people. I could have told them about the time during that summer in Hot Springs when, returning to the city after a day's drive in the country, we stopped to take in the view. Prairielanders that we were, we had never until that summer in the Ozarks seen a mountain —hardly anything that could be called a hill. As we rounded a bend we saw ahead of and far below us the lights of the city just beginning to twinkle like the first few fireflies of the evening. My father pulled the car onto the margin of the road and switched off the engine and the headlights. We watched in silence as dusk settled and the scintillance spread. We might have happened onto the hidden valley where the falling stars all fell.

We did not see the approaching car until it was upon us, for despite the duskiness, it was being driven without lights. It was going very slowly, which turned out to be our salvation, but which in the meantime lent an eerie clarity and a slow-motion suspense to what we saw happening to us that made it all the more apparition-like and nightmarish. Already the car was failing to follow the bend in the road, straying out of its lane and into the other one—ours. Still with no correction in its course, it rolled on straight toward us. It was a pick-up truck, a farm truck, far heavier than our car, and we were parked not more than a yard from the edge of a precipice where there was no wall, no rail, nothing to keep us from being knocked off and plunging two hundred feet.

My father had now switched on our headlights and was pushing on the horn. It was in that glare and to that frantic sound that the crash came. I was thrown from one side of the back seat to the other. My mother found her voice and screamed.

I reopened my eyes to find that we were still where we had been. The truck, its engine stalled, sat straddling the road. My father was already out of his door.

He strode through the light to the cab of the truck, yanked open the driver's door and reached inside with both hands. He dragged out a man who seemed to be still half asleep and not to know what had or what was happening to him. Holding him by the bib of his overalls, my father hit him full in the face. He must have broken the man's nose, for blood flew into the air, spattering him. He had certainly knocked him unconscious, for he had to hold him to hit him again. He hit him again and yet again as he sagged. And when the man was dead weight in his grip he held him just off the ground and hit him again and again and again. I could hear the blows when I could no longer bear to watch. It was the sound my mother made when she pounded a piece of meat to make it tender.

My father let go and dropped the man to the pavement. He got into the truck, started it and parked it on the embankment behind our car. He dragged the unconscious man there by the straps of his overalls. We drove into Hot Springs without a word. The light of the dashboard cast shadows into my father's pallid face that made it look skeletal. Blood shone on the knuckles of his right hand. His ulcer, as we learned the next day, had just perforated.

That was what my father—now that he had had to quit drinking himself—did to drunken drivers who endangered his wife and child. "Good thing for you all he doesn't know what you're thinking about him!" I could have told my mother's people.

THEY HAD ALWAYS DISAPPROVED of my father. The Varleys did not much approve of anybody who was not a Varley, but of all their sons-in-law, daughters-, brothers-, sisters-in-law, they disapproved of him the most—had right from the start. The Varleys held themselves a cut above their distant neighbors, the Humphreys. Or rather, two cuts; one cut they held themselves above all their neighbors, and all of *them* held themselves a cut above the Humphreys. Ed Varley might not own an acre of land more than Will Humphrey did, but he rented his; he was not a sharecropper. Rented the same piece of land, there in Sherry, year after year; the Varleys did not pick up and move every fall as soon as crops were gathered and sold, restless as a band of Gipsies. They were settled, stable, respectable people, in debt to nobody. They had raised—including the three left him by his first wife—twelve children. They saw them all through four grades of school before putting them to work—even the girls. Theirs were brought up to mind their parents. The disrespect of those three little Humphrey hellions for theirs had been the scandal of four neighboring communities, and that Clarence was the worst of the trio. Him they could do nothing with, and before long that mother of his gave up even trying, even caring. The man had been plain to see already in the boy. Now, as then, as often as not, he was off with a gun lazing around in the woods—if you were to believe just half of what you heard said, then it would be as well if he spent all his time there. Stories of brawls, fist-fights when the bootleg liquor flowed at country dances, on the square in Clarksville on Saturday nights, of scenes in public with girls he had trifled with, of brushes with the law and of doings which ought to have involved him with the law but had not—not yet. Rumors that his work on cars was not always to keep them running. That, for a share of the insurance money, he could rig the wiring and the gasoline tank in such a way . . . Well, some of this was no doubt exaggerated, even untrue, unfair. But there was no smoke without fire. The point was, he was the sort about whom stories circulated.

He was too little to be good, too cocky for his size—a fellow who somehow deprived a tall man of his natural advantage and made *him* feel ill-at-ease, feel that this one very likely carried brass knuckles in his pocket or a switchblade to cut you down to size. He was vain, took a little too much care of his person, was a shade too well groomed. His white teeth and his black eyes sparkled a bit too brightly. He had an air of knowing more about you, and caring less, than you knew about yourself. "A little bantam rooster," Ed Varley called him.

Even if he had had a more savory reputation, however, he was invading a very close-knit family (something he would hardly even recognize when he saw it, coming from the one he did) in the Varleys. One where obedience was not demanded but freely given, and one in which the parents were more than usually reluctant to see their children leave home. The one he was after was her father's favorite, the pet of them all. He was about as welcome as a fox in a henhouse.

I SPEAK OF WHAT I SAW FOR MYSELF. So I must do, for I was never told very much. It was my misfortune to be an inquisitive child and to have two taciturn, practically tonguetied, grandfathers, and for each of them to have an exotic background that further piqued my curiosity. I have spoken already of my untalkative part-Indian grandfather Humphrey. My grandfather Varley was as stingy with his words as if he were composing a telegram, and he was an Englishman, a full-blooded Englishman, born—this shows how little over the years I was ever able to get out of him—in Leicester or in Leeds, I am not sure which, as long ago as 1856—a man who must have seen many strange and interesting sights, who must remember many ways and things now changed and gone. His coming to America—to found our line—was straight out of a storybook. He was only a boy when his older brother, a dandy, a fop, ordered him to black his boots one day. My grandfather proudly refused. His brother cuffed him. He complained to their father. Their father cuffed him for complaining. He ran away. He walked to London from Leicester or from Leeds, there signed on and served as cabin-boy on a sailing ship bound for Galveston.

This totally satisfying first chapter must, surely, have been followed by a second? It could not be, as it seemed to me, that the next and only other thing he did was to start breeding—although, to be sure, the number (three by his dead first wife, nine by my grandmother) would scarcely have left him time for much else.

His love of children extended no further than to those of his own get; for his grandchildren he had about as much feeling as a cucumber has for its. But he was the best father who ever lived—this was the first article of faith in my mother's family: that theirs was the best father, and the best husband, who ever lived—though, in contrast to his love of children, which ended with his own, his perfection as a husband only began on the second try, with my grandmother. For she was the Rachel to his first wife's Leah: that was article number two of the faith of my mother's family. To them it was no disparagement of their father to think that while he might have married two women he had loved only one.

The selfless devotion, the constant affection of their parents for each other, even after all these years, was as tireless as that of a pair of lovebirds in a cage. To their daughters, that long love affair was a delight, a running entertainment which they followed like a daily radio serial, reporting to one another any episodes that might have been missed; to their sons it was an example; to all it was an inspiration. They would all gather round to watch her wrap him in a sheet up to his collar, whet the razor on the strop, work up a lather in the mug and lather his face and shave him (he had never once shaved himself in his life—did not know how) with the pleasure of children at the zoo watching one monkey pluck the fleas out of its mate's fur. If only, thought those of the girls who were married, if only their marriages had been like that! At least they had the satisfaction of knowing that they were the products of a perfect union.

Never were two people more contented with each other, certainly not two people married to each other. That, after all their years together, she still called him

"Mister Varley," not even "Edward," much less "Ed," did not indicate any reserve or inequality between them; that usage was common among their generation in that part of the world, and was intended to instill respect for the father in the children. What a contrast they were to my other grandparents! Catch Net Humphrey mistering her Will! She was barely civil to him, much less respectful. Catch her shaving him! Sooner cut his throat.

I could never get much out of my grandmother Varley either. She was too concerned for my grandfather's welfare to have much time for me. With so many grandchildren, she never had much time for any of them. Sometimes it seemed to me she hardly knew one from another, or that she even tried very hard to keep them straight. She always needed reminding of any of our little differences and tastes.

She enjoyed a reputation as a witch, but about this she was not talkative—indeed, she was positively sibylline. People came to her from miles around to have her remove warts by spells and charms. At this she was infallible. Clairvoyance was attributed to her. She hinted at possessing occult powers. She could make you think she had read your fortune, and that it was not a very good one, when you were on a course that in some way displeased or inconvenienced her. While she did not claim to have had converse with spirits, she did not explicitly deny that she had. None of which trafficking in the black arts gave her the least doubt that she was bound for Heaven, that her place there was reserved and waiting. She spoke of it as though she had already inspected and approved it, like those senior citizens given trips to Florida by realtors to pick out their retirement homes. She spoke of Hell, too, as though she had once passed through; her descriptions were as graphic as color slides. Her notion of an engaging conversation was whether we retained our bodily senses and appetites in the hereafter. Was there food in Heaven, music, night and day? Being unresolvable, such questions were inexhaustible. I wondered once as we sat on the porch in the dusk after supper talking about Heaven, what we would do for conversation once we were there and knew all there was to know about it.

One metaphysical question that vexed my grandmother, which was never discussed but which was in the air for all to feel at such times, was whether in Heaven she would have to share her husband with that first wife of his. Such was her jealousy of that long-dead woman, despite all her husband's devotion to herself, that her name was never pronounced; I never learned what it was. I always felt that my grandmother's fecundity—nine to three, her favor, was the final score between her and her rival—was her way of establishing the better eternal claim to her Mr. Varley.

Meanwhile, in this vale of tears, what she liked best to do was to fish. Her partner in this—and she had to have a partner, an accomplice—was her neighbor down the road, Mrs. Exom. Mrs. Exom lived to fish. Much fun was made, behind her back, of Mrs. Exom and her fishing, as it is of anyone who turns a pastime into a passion —no one made more fun of her than my grandmother, whose passion for fishing was every bit as great as hers. Mrs. Exom would come down the road enveloped in her ground-length gingham dress and wearing her huge straw hat that made her look like some large species of toadstool, her cane pole over her shoulder, her minnow bucket in her hand, and the sight of her would set my grandmother's head shaking in a mixture of amusement, pity and contempt. However, she never let her pass without hailing her. At first it would be, "Me? Oh, law' no, Mrs. Exom! *I* can't just drop all I've got waiting for me to do and go off fishing. Who would iron all those clothes I've got sprinkled? Who would churn that butter?" But there was always a daughter to iron the clothes, a boy to churn the butter, and Mrs. Exom—well, as my grandmother said, she just wouldn't take no for an answer; the only way to get rid of her was to give in to her. On afternoons in the summer during my visits to the farm when, for some reason, despite my grandmother's derisive predictions, her eager lookout, Mrs. Exom did not come down the road, then I would be called in from whatever I was entertaining myself with, told that I was bored with having nothing to do and that what all boys liked, as she very well knew, was to go fishing (I hated fishing—sitting on a creek bank by the hour dangling a line in the water—hated it even when the fish were biting) and, with the sigh of a woman for the incorrigible boyishness of males of all ages, she would volunteer to sacrifice her afternoon and take me, on condition that I dig the worms.

Being so content with each other, my grandparents were, naturally, content with what they had jointly produced: their children. Not that they boasted of their worldly attainments or their brilliant matches, for, indeed, there was nothing like that to boast of. But— and this was all that mattered—they were good children. Good *children*, that is to say—meaning, good to their old parents. Their old parents were grateful, and told them so. Each giving the other all the credit ("You don't know how lucky you are to have your mammy," he was forever telling them; and she told them they had the best father, and she the best husband, in the world) they praised their children to their faces, constantly. It would have taken a monster of contrariness to disappoint or disillusion them.

Theirs was the only family anywhere near as large that seemed not to have cost the parents any self-sacrifice whatever. They were not Catholics, not even very churchy Protestants, yet they seemed to have obeyed joyfully some Pope's injunction to abstain from abstention, to be fruitful and multiply, and increase the number of God's faithful. Or rather, it would have seemed like that had it not seemed that the gods they had trained their children to revere were themselves, and that the number of them ensured that, as one grew up and flew the nest, another was ripe to take his place at the plow, her place in the kitchen.

Their children admired everything about their parents, but what they admired the most was the self-denial of both, the total devotion of one to the other. Each was absolutely indifferent to personal comfort and well-being, concerned entirely and constantly for that of the other. Neither ever asked for a thing. Instead, "Go see if your mammy wants anything," he was forever saying, just as she was forever saying, "Take such and such to your father—you know he will never ask for it." He impatiently, even angrily, rejected any effort to pamper him—almost as if to do so were somehow to neglect their mother, and she was just the same, only, of course, in reverse. "Give that to your mammy," he would say sternly, reprovingly, as he refused the choice cut of the meat. "No, Mr. Varley," she would say, "I insist that you have it." It was only to please the other that both gave in and agreed to share it. Their children looked on adoringly. They loved the way they spoiled each other, and never realized it was they themselves who were used by both in doing it. You had to be a generation removed from it to see it as it was. Then it was apparent even to a child.

Without each other, both would surely have perished of self-neglect; but, as they had each other, and had that corps (I am tempted to say, that crop which they had reaped) of manservants and handmaidens, their children, each to command to wait upon the other, they both got looked after like royalty. Meanwhile, the pair of them seated in the two best chairs, each with a pillow, both with footstools and slippers, he with his tin can to spit in, she with hers (he chewed tobacco, she dipped snuff), twin haloes of self-abnegation shone above their silvery heads.

HE SEEMED TO HAVE NOTICED, all right, but to have decided to excuse them for the cool reception the Varleys gave him when he came courting their Nell. As though he had gotten the message, but, having glanced at the envelope and seen whom it was from, he had thrown it away unopened. He made himself welcome, overlooking their ungraciousness as though not wanting to embarrass them by drawing attention to their bad manners.

He drove out from Clarksville—he had left home when he was little more than a boy, lived in town in bachelor's quarters (everybody knew what that meant) —on Sunday afternoons, proclaiming his coming by the dust he raised all along the road. He would sit behind the wheel for a moment after he had reined up at the gate to let the dust settle. Then out he swaggered. There was about him an air of accounting himself a new sort of man, one of a new age, the age of speed, of the automobile, amused by and slyly patronizing toward those whom he had superseded, the slow, older sort, the horse-drawn ones, like Ed Varley, for example.

That machine which delivered him to the gate was enough in itself to rouse Ed Varley's mistrust, dislike, fear. He recognized it for what it was: the vehicle of change. It brought to Sherry, to his own doorstep, a tremor of that seismic upheaval which, since the war, was shaking the world. The restlessness, the wayward-ness of youth, their flight from parental authority, the wide scattering of families; the automobile symbolized all this, it was the actual instrument of it, and the impudent little bugger, up from nowhere, who came sauntering out of that one of his, whose trade it was to fix the things, personified this onslaught of mechaniza-tion which threatened to disrupt and replace all that was familiar, comprehensible, easygoing.

It was plain to see that he had not come from church in those duds. When you knew—as everyone did know, whom did he think he was fooling?—what he came from, what he was, then that straw boater he wore was even more of an impudence, the angle at which he set it provoking enough to make a man want to knock it off his head. He seemed to be just daring you to do that.

All smiles, all politeness, all compliments (so that later, when they found fault with him, she could contrast his gentlemanliness toward them) he could not be made to feel unwelcome. And there was something about him which kept you from telling him to his face that he was, from ordering him off the place. Odd that such a little runt of a man could give that impression. Or was that so odd, after all? His being little was what made it dangerous to cross him.

Besides, as they could see to their dismay and despair, the child was infatuated with him. Always such a good girl—he seemed to have brought out a devil in her. Their opposition to him brought it out, too. They could only hope that he would soon tire of her—and hope that in the meantime she was mindful of her up-bringing, of her family's unsullied name.

They soon decided that they had been wrong about one thing. It was not that he was unaware of bringing dissension into a family unused to any. It was not that his own made him unable to imagine a family like theirs. He understood very well what his coming had disturbed. Out of spite for never having had a decent harmonious home-life of his own, he enjoyed upsetting theirs. He enjoyed setting child against parent, as he had always set himself against his own. It brought out all the mis-chief in him, to show Ed Varley his influence over her father's favorite.

He had picked the one child in that otherwise well-regimented family who was used to having her own way. Surely it pained them the most, but just as surely they were more tolerant of her independence now than they would have been of that of any other of their children. It was their Nell whom they could never deny, never gainsay. She had always been given special considera-tion—was more than a little spoiled by them all. Since that accident to her hand when she was only three, she had always been excused from the rougher farm chores expected of the other girls and given the daintier tasks to do. Her older sisters and brothers pampered and petted her as much as her parents did, for they blamed themselves for what had happened.

It happened at haymaking time. The children frolicked in the hay as the workhands pitched it by the forkful into the wagonbed. When the wagon was full, they rode on top of the hay back to the barn. There the wagon was drawn inside and the team unhitched. They were then driven outside and harnessed to a rope which, running through a pulley attached to the roofbeam, lifted the hay into the loft with a large pair of tongs. The children's game was to grab hold of the rope and ride to the rooftop, then let go and fall into the haypile.

They could get away with it because their father was outside driving the team and could not see them. They had been forbidden to do it, told that it was dangerous. But it was not dangerous. They had been doing it for years—all except little Nell—without any of them getting hurt. Though the drop was long, the landing in the hay was as soft as in a feather bed. You just had to let go in time, was all. Otherwise your hands could get drawn into the pulley. Until that last possible moment you held on. For the higher you rode, the farther the fall, the bigger the thrill.

"Try it, Nell," they said. "It's fun." But the little one was afraid.

"Watch me!" said her brother, and grabbed the rope and rose into the air, let go and fell back into the hay and came up laughing.

So she tried it.

"Let go!" they yelled.

"I'm afraid!" she cried.

"Let go!" they screamed.

But the higher she rose the more terrified she was and the tighter she held on. She fell, unconscious, when the pulley severed her grip. She lost the middle finger of her right hand down to the root. The ring finger was permanently stiffened half-closed. The palm was mangled.

She was allowed to begin earlier than most little girls to play the little lady, and as part of her dressing up she wore gloves much of the time, summer and winter. But it was not just the gloves that kept most people from ever guessing that anything was wrong with her. The right hand was kept out of sight, yet so naturally that it was never missed. It was the one that worked below the quilt or the hoop whenever she was quilting or embroidering. She perfected a way of crossing her index finger over the stump of the missing one that hid the stump, even when she was cutting her meat at table. The best proof of her dexterity, when barehanded, at concealing her disfigurement by holding the bad hand in the good one or carrying a handkerchief always crumpled in it, was that my father had been married to her for five years before he learned about it—and my father was not an unobservant man. For all the bathing of me that she did, for all the countless times I watched her kneading dough, shelling peas, plucking fowls, I was eight years old before I spied it.

So for Nell a special case was made. Instead of being sent to Sherry's nearby one-room schoolhouse, where all her brothers and sisters had gone, she was driven daily in the wagon for her four years the seven miles to and from Clarksville's grammar school. There she was taught to write left-handed, and there she was made to feel that although she was a country girl, she was no ordinary one, but was, in fact, already rather refined. It was she who was called upon most often to read and recite, she whose pronunciation the other pupils were urged to imitate. For the teachers were all strong anglophiles, and she had picked up from her English father his way of talking, had kept it by not playing much with other children. That, in his native England, her father's accent alone would have given him away as irredeemably lower class, no one in Clarksville had any way of knowing.

Having had that taste of town life, she found life in the country afterwards monotonous, constricted and coarse. She was determined to live in town. It could be done. She had before her the examples of her oldest brother and her oldest sister. Herbert was the manager of a five and ten cent store in Corsicana. Being a woman, she could not hope for anything like that, of course. Her sister Gertrude, after the death of both her husband and her baby daughter in the influenza epidemic, had gone to Dallas, trained as a stenographer and typist, supported herself. With her hand, she could not do that, either. What she could do was not marry a farmboy.

So when Clarence Humphrey came calling on her he had something already going for him. She liked that car and the confidence with which he handled it. She liked that sailor's straw hat and the tilt at which he wore it. She liked that sassy smile. She liked the fact that he seemed to think rather well of himself—what woman wants a man who does not? And that was what he made her, for the first time in all her sixteen years, feel like: a woman—no longer a girl. She was flattered to have attracted a man—a man of twenty-three, not another pimply boy. One who lived in town and had town ways and manners, not a gawky plowhand who tripped over his tongue and blushed to be looked at as though ashamed of what was going through his mind.

He took her to Sunday baseball games around the county. She quickly grasped the rules, learned to appreciate fine plays, soon was as avid a fan as he was. He taught her to shoot a rifle, made a crack shot out of her. Much of their courtship was spent at that still novel pleasure, driving. She enjoyed tearing along the dusty roads in his open touring car. She had ridden a few times in cars before, but seldom in the front seat, never as the sole passenger. She, too, she found, liked speed—admired his mastery over it. He taught her to drive. She was an apt pupil, was soon almost as good a driver as he was—and just as fast.

Going with him gave her a glimpse of what exciting times she was living in. The telephone, the phonograph, the motion pictures, the first radios, above all the automobile were reaching everywhere, and nothing would ever be the same again. Her generation were striking off old shackles, living life with a freedom and fun never known before. It was exciting—for a country girl, one raised as strictly as she, it was sometimes a little frightening: bootleg liquor, cigarettes, bobbing your hair as a gesture of emancipation. It all went to your head. Once you had had a taste of it, you wanted more. As the song they were singing that year went, "How you gonna keep 'em down on the farm after they've seen Paree?" Clarksville was not Paree, but it was sure a lot livelier than Sherry!

This new pace of life was just his speed. He was always going somewhere, and always in a hurry, and he was never at a loss for somewhere to go, something entertaining to do. He was like a boy out of school—the day was never long enough for him. "Let's go swimming! Hurry! There's a tentshow in town—Let's go! Let's have a picnic! Let's—" There was never a dull moment with him.

They criticized him to her for the very qualities she liked in him. That he was carefree and laughter-loving. That here he was, now twenty-four years old and still always playing, never serious-minded. That he would never grow up, settle down. She said, "What's that to me?" They said, "Well! If you're not thinking seriously about him then you're spending far too much time with him, young lady!" And she said, "Well, it's because he's fun to be with." What she did not say was that she wanted never to settle down either. He had shown her what fun life could be, and she saw no more reason than he did why the fun should ever stop. She had no intention, when all her dancing was through, of settling into a cottage for two, learning to cook and to sew— what's more, to love it, I know—and being his or anybody else's stay-at-home, play-at-home, nine-o'clock- sleepytime gal.

It was this that he had uncovered—or had himself instilled—in her, this that drew him to her. "You're like me," he told her. "Another redhead, like me." (For in those days, before time had darkened it, his hair was still red.) "We're all alike. All restless. All wild. All hellers, all of us."

He uncovered a streak of jealousy in her, too. He

liked that, liked seeing it flash, liked knowing that he himself had sparked it. "I like 'em hot," he said. It was how he liked everything: hot and spicy. If the spice was lacking, he added it. Just the opposite of Ed Varley, at whose table, by whose order, no spice, not even salt and pepper, was ever allowed.

She was a jealous woman—a regular spitfire; she herself said so. Said so not as though it was a sin or a fault of character, something to be kept hidden and fought against, but something to brag about.

In this she was following the example that had been set her, as well as the custom of the country. It was the thing she most admired in her mother, her jealousy of her husband, and she admired it all the more for its purity, which is to say, its pointlessness; for that model of uxoriousness, Ed Varley, had never given his wife cause for a single one of the countless pangs she had suffered over him—which in itself must have caused her the sharpest pang of all, for it suggested to her mind that he had been just as singly attached to that dead first wife of his, who was the woman of whom she was jealous.

To my mother, not to be jealous of your man was not to love him; not to be ready to kill him if he two-timed you was to belittle him. When told she ought to be ashamed of her jealous nature, she replied that she could not help herself, she was born that way. The fieriness of her temper came to her naturally; she was a redhead, and all redheaded women were born wildcats. The gory details she went into of what she would do to both parties if ever some other woman. . . ! In this, my mother was not alone; indeed, she was merely chanting an old refrain. *He was her man, but he done her wrong*—and

what Frankie then did to Johnny was what was expected
of her, fabled in folklore, sanctioned in song.

WHEN, BY THE STEADINESS OF HIS ATTENTIONS to her,
he could no longer be denied the right to keep her out
at night, they began going to country dances. It was as
if he were an Indian going back to his reservation for a
tribal dance. It was to Lone Star, his old stamping
grounds, that he took her. There, just next door to her
own, was a world unknown to her—almost another race.

They drove down dirt roads cut like trenches through
the solid trees. Coons and foxes crossing the road were
a commoner sight than people. Skins of others of them
were stretched on the sides of the barns behind the rare
houses, where cars passed so seldom that, to watch
theirs, the entire family would be waiting on the porch
or out in the yard. If he stopped to chat, the children
shied and hid like little animals. Telephones—even
postal service—being unheard-of, one wondered how,
short of smoke signals, word was ever gotten out of this
wilderness that somebody was having a dance—unless
they fell on certain moons, like annual tribal observ-
ances. One was prompted to such thoughts because
evidence lingered on in many faces of some early
mingling with the Indians in the depths of these woods,
before the Indians were dispossessed and driven across
the river into Oklahoma.

When they got there it would seem that they had
come to the wrong place. No dance here tonight. The
people in this house were busy at that very moment
moving out. Armchairs and rockers, a table, a buffet

sat in the yard, and two men were bringing out a rolled-up rug. The wagons and teams seemed waiting to be loaded with the contents of the house. He at once, or rather, after a welcoming tumblerful of white whiskey, joined in this work, which went on, joined in by new arrivals, and fuelled by more whiskey, until a room of the house had been entirely emptied for the dancing.

Babysitting—even the word for it—being a thing unknown there in those times, children were taken wherever their parents went. In a room—often the only other room—that had not been emptied, they were all put together in however many beds there were, the smaller ones in the bed under the bed: the trundle-bed. Once they were all tucked in, the music was struck up.

The first number was apt to be the old waltz called "Over the Wave," for that was Clarence's favorite tune, and the musicians—the same two who would play it at his funeral—were his father and his only uncle, Joe Sample. They were the professionals. Among the crowd there was sure to be somebody who played the French harp—as they called the harmonica. Some played it uncommonly well, but as the instrument was so common, it was not admitted to the band on a footing with the fiddles, and the player of it went unpaid. Then maybe, in her honor, they would render, "I Was Seeing Nellie Home."

They played "After the Ball Is Over," "I Dreamt that I Dwelt in Marble Halls," "Flow Gently, Sweet Afton," "Drink to Me Only with Thine Eyes"—songs with words, songs they shared with people in the outside world, and for these the older women, who needed a little but not much coaxing, were led onto the floor.

The rhythm quickened. Waltzes and the measures

trodden to them gave way to sprightlier tunes. The temperature rose, faces reddened. Through the screenless windows and the open doors moths came to cloud the coal-oil lamps that flickered on the walls. Resting between numbers, the women chatted on the moonlit porch, hummed the tunes they had heard played. The men excused themselves and disappeared, all down the same path, into the darkness of the woods. The harsh homemade whiskey discharged a current through the veins like an electric shock.

Faster music was called for. The bows sawed the strings. Yet the faces of the fiddlers never changed expression—that is to say, they remained as blank of expression as ever, as though it would have been unbecoming for them to seem to enjoy their playing, like a man's laughing at his own joke. The dancers grew younger, the older people sitting out the numbers, beginning to go home. The stamp of feet shook the walls. There were cries and calls—"Whew! Whew! Yea-hoo!" The floor cleared for one couple, then another, to show off their fastest step, to keep it up for as long as they could.

After a rest—after more whiskey—back to it. And' now a new note entered into the music, one that the dancers seemed to have been waiting for, something all their own, like some tribal dance known only to those of the blood, who had passed through their rites of initiation, and which roused their most basic feelings. Faster and faster it went. A wild wail was in it, and underneath the wail, a drone, a skirl. The fiddles had become bagpipes. It was, indeed, the music of their clan, and produced in them the emotions that "The Campbells Are Coming" produces in those of that company.

Clarence Humphrey felt a tap on his shoulder. He

looked up into the face of a man who said, "I'm cutting in."

"The hell you say," said Clarence.

"All right with you if I cut in, Nell?" the man asked.

"It's for Clarence to say," she said.

"Hell-fire, you're not married to him."

The music stopped. The dancers turned, seeking the cause. The room fell into sudden silence.

"It's for Clarence to say," she said.

"I say, 'No,' " he said. "If you've got anything more to say, let's step outside."

"No, Clarence! No!" she said.

The other men all accompanied them outdoors, to watch and to referee. The women closed around her. She cried over what she had caused. The women consoled her, but in fact they envied her; and while they understood her tears, that she was obliged to shed them, they took it for granted that they were hypocritical.

He was back in a quarter of an hour, the strong smell of victory on his breath. One of his eyes was closed, both his cheekbones skinned and swollen, his grin crooked and split, his knuckles raw. But of the two of them, he alone came back. He had chased his rival from the field.

"Oh, how awful!" she said, seeing his wounds, and she meant it, but she said it with pride. "You fool! You little fool, you!" she said adoringly.

Now, more than half a century later, here am I, one product of that night, writing about it.

Bodies and brains heated by fast fiddle music and wild dancing; a spark of jealousy igniting the vapors of strong, illicit whiskey; a challenge given and accepted; a bare-knuckled bout by moonlight; these were elements in my begetting—and they might just as easily not have been. Having fought over her, having fought and whipped a man bigger than himself, he might have reckoned he had a right to claim his reward that night. After what he had done for her, and being only seventeen, could she have refused him? Or would she then have refused ever to see him again? Would he, if he had gotten his way, have wanted any more than that of her? Upon such tricky turning points does our coming into the world depend. It was his having fought over her that preserved her both from him and from herself. It had raised them both in his regard. She was now too precious, he himself too gallant to do anything other than what he did.

She said, "Yes," and, in the spring of 1922, both said, "I do," and set up house in Clarksville—in that house where, two years later, I was born, that mysterious, tantalizing, lost house, which not only vanished from the face of the earth, taking with it the charmed life it had sheltered, but taking with it also into limbo, for all that I could learn otherwise, the very plot of earth on which it had stood.

V

LATER IN THE MORNING my father's parents were brought in from the country to join us on the Paris hospital grounds.

As always, it was impossible to tell what my grandfather was feeling—whether he was feeling anything new to him. His face had the range of expression of a tombstone: rain or shine, its somber inscription the same. He bore this new blow as he had borne a lifetime of them, with the same unflinching patience as his old plowhorse bore the whip, and plodded on at the only pace he knew. One could draw no comfort from his outward evenness, for it was not the sign of inner composure or fortitude but of resignation, of settled despondency—perhaps, by now, of numbness. He came wearing his suit—an ominous signal to me, for, except to church, he never wore it but to funerals—and his better hat. The hat—black felt, despite the heat of the summer day—remained just as it had come from its box long years ago: the tall crown round, undented, the broad brim flat—still waiting for an owner to impart to it his preference, his personality.

His handshake was as limp and lifeless as ever (I never kissed his cheek, as I always did my other grandfather's, on instructions from my mother): the hand feverish to the touch from the years of exposure and hard usage, and incapable of closing or opening fully, like a rusty, stiff, old hinge. How with hands like his he could finger his fiddle was a wonder to me.

My grandmother was all tears. This now from the son who had never brought her anything but trouble! Who better than she had always known it would come to something like this one day? Foreseeing the worst, she was inconsolable, and bitter in advance at not getting the pity which was her due.

It was one of the very few times I had ever seen my two sets of grandparents together, for, needless to say, the disapproval of my father which they shared was no bond between them. It was so unnatural a meeting that it frightened me in itself. Seeing them both before me, I resented them both, his parents for their mistreatment of him as a boy, hers for their disapproval of him. The image of my mother and me left to their forebearance came to me, and I prayed, "Oh, God, please, please, don't let my father die!"

IT WAS MY FIRST TIME inside one of those worlds within a world: a hospital. Our injuries and our illnesses until now had been minor enough to be treated in doctors' offices. Entering the building was a dislocation which reminded me of stepping from the busy square into the picture-show where a silent film was already half unreeled, or of plunging inside the frosty and silent cold-storage plant on a hot, bright summer day. The corridors down which we were led, white and bare of decoration, were like chutes. People hurried along them silently or speaking low, the staff members in squeaky rubber-soled shoes, the visitors on tiptoe. This combination of silence and urgency heightened the air of suspense. At our passage, the patients in their beds in the wards turned listless, incurious faces at us. Even more frightening were those who did not turn to look but stared on at the ceiling. Outside the closed doors, in clusters that detached them from even the life of this separate and self-enclosed world, stood relatives of the patient inside, their faces stricken, their eyes tearful. Already the smell of ether in the hall was nauseating me and making me fear that I would shame myself by throwing up.

Nothing before had ever been so real as this unreality. Yesterday you were unaware of this silent but hectic place; now, within seconds, it was your world, where, suspended between hope and dread, you would concentrate your life until you were discharged to resume the one you had checked at the door, or to start an entirely new one.

We were shown, through a window, a mummy, and told that it was my father. He was entirely wrapped in bandages. What had been done for him was little. Some surface lacerations stitched, some broken bones set, but his most serious injuries were internal, and what to do about these was still under consideration. I had my first premonition that my father was going to die.

I HAD ONLY A PASSING ACQUAINTANCE with death. I myself had died once (I had—or had had until it was destroyed—a document in testimony of the fact); but, aside from that one brief personal encounter, only one other time had death ever struck anywhere within my view. Nobody in my family, big as it was, had died in my lifetime. I knew only one person who had had a death in his family: Martin Scaffe, and that had happened before I knew Martin. I had known just one person who died. This death touched me, though not closely. But it did touch me, because he was a boy I knew, one my own age, a classmate of mine, because he died in the same way I myself had come so close to doing that I was given up for dead, and because I had business dealings with him at the time of his death.

I got into business because my means were proving insufficient to my wants. I had tried the system, newly imported among us Clarksville boys, of having my mother put me on a weekly allowance. This I budgeted. Having a budget to keep within only increased my wants. I could finagle more out of the old, loose, non-contract, paternalistic arrangement. Whenever my mother took herself firmly in hand and denied me something for my own good, I could always go down to the shop and wheedle it out of my father.

But there was a limit to what I dared ask him for. Times were hard. If I was to have some of the things I longed for, I must earn some money.

One Saturday afternoon I borrowed the family lawnmower and pushed it off down the street. Writing now, it is necessary to say that this was not a powered mower. It was a blazing June afternoon. I asked a boy-less neighbor, upon whom I shall here and now at last wreak my vengeance not by naming him but by leaving him forever as nameless as a cur, if he would like his lawn mowed. It surely needed it. While I mowed it, the man lolled in the shade of his front porch reading and sipping iced tea. It was a good-sized lawn. I, undersized then as always, began to realize before I was halfway done with it that I was not up to the job. Pushing the mower through the rank grass strained my abdomen, made me sick at my stomach. The job took me three hours. When I got done I was fever-hot. My work was inspected and found passable. My neighbor asked how much he owed me.

Following my mother's instructions, I replied, "Whatever you please, sir," and held out my sweaty little palm.

In it was put a dime.

Following my mother's instructions, and choking back my tears of disappointment and anger, I thanked the man.

As I was struggling home, I met the evening paper boy on his route. We accompanied each other down the street, I pushing the lawnmower while he folded his papers and sailed them onto the front porches of his subscribers. His looked to me like pleasant work. Well, if I thought I would like it, another of the carriers, P. J. Jones, wanted to sell his route.

P.J. wanted five dollars for his paper route. That was a lot more money than I could raise at one go. P.J. agreed to let me pay him off in installments.

My paper route took me into the only section of Clarksville with which I was still unfamiliar: Niggertown. Now on the map of my home town I had colored in all the parts.

I had paid him three of the five dollars I owed him when P. J. Jones, aged eleven, drowned while swimming that summer. Unlike me, P.J. drowned for good.

His was the first death among the children my age. None of us felt it very keenly; I mainly felt how lucky I had been. None of us knew P.J. very well. At school, during recess, on the playground, he had kept to himself. A so-so pupil, he was unnoticeable in class; in fact, to get by unnoticed there appeared to be P.J.'s hope. Poorer than most of the rest of us, he had had no time after school or on Saturdays for play. He had carried the paper route because he really needed the money. He had sold it because he needed something to bring him in more money than it did.

It brought in little, as I soon learned. In fact, I lost on it. In fact, P.J. had skinned me. But business was business. To the heirs of the late P. J. Jones I owed two dollars.

I had to ask whereabouts in town P.J. had lived. I was not much surprised to learn that it was in the section behind Silk Stocking Street—well behind it— west of the high school: a poor section even by my standards, isolated and at a long distance from everywhere else. After letting a month go by following the death, I went to pay P.J.'s mother the balance I owed for the paper route.

I did not know Mrs. Jones, but I feared that she might know who I was. That she might have heard that old story about me. To me it was so important that I could hardly believe there was anybody in town who did not know it—she, now, least of all. It made me unique. Would she remember and recognize me as the boy who had come so close to dying the same death her boy had died?

It was the still middle of a glaring, suffocatingly hot summer day. Above the pavement heat waves shimmered like water. My walk, up west Washington Street, was long and steep. My memory stalked beside me as unshakeable as my shadow, reminding me with each step of those moments on a similar day four years earlier. It was the most vivid of all my memories and little was ever needed to transport me back to that time; never had it been so vivid, so oppressive as now.

It had had, while it was happening, the quality of a dream, one of those that the sleeper knows is a dream but cannot wake from, struggles to rise from only to sink back helplessly time after time. In memory it had retained the hallucinatory sharpness that only a dream can have, and that maddening persistency, that tenacity of a dream, due in part to its very incommunicability, to the knowledge that you must live alone with it for life, that you can never exorcise any portion of it by making another person really see it, and thus become co-owner of it with you. Only one other person of my lifelong acquaintance would have understood: the dead P. J. Jones. Now on this dreamlike, almost comatose day, this day of almost subaqueous silence, it all came flooding back over me.

By the time I reached the Joneses' house I had lost the sensation of walking and felt that I was floating— or rather, sinking. I was dizzied, almost dazed, by the rippling, palpitant heat waves. Things swam in my sight. I panted for breath. The heat and my own mounting fear bathed me in sweat as cold and copious as a pool. I longed for my mother, and this longing made me reject the very thought of any other woman but her. The last one on earth I wanted to see right now was the woman whose door I had just knocked on.

One glimpse of her and I knew I had ventured into depths over my head, into the adult world of profound human sorrow. The month that had passed since her loss had dispelled none of the vague, stunned look on her face, the timorousness of her movements and the continual flinching as though in expectation of some crushing new blow which I in my turn was to learn is the effect of sudden, accidental bereavement. She winced at the sight of me—not necessarily because I was who I was; as I was also to learn, one winces at such times at the sight of anybody at all, for half of oneself then lies newly buried and the surviving half is still too tender and raw to bear the touch of an eye. No doubt to Mrs. Jones the sight of a boy the age of her own was doubly painful—one who had known him, as she had, but who would not miss him as she would. Here was I, come to pay what I owed for the paper route her boy had once carried. I wished the earth would open up and swallow me. At the same time I longed to have her hug me to her breast, to reassure me that I was alive and safe, and to forgive me for being so.

I murmured my name, then while I was still trying to muster the words to state my errand, Mrs. Jones invited me to come in. I did not want to go inside but I saw that I was in too deep to buy my way out quickly and cheaply. I walked under the arm with which she held the screen door open for me.

She asked would I like a glass of lemonade and I said yes instead of no because there was a look of such earnest entreaty on her face. It was already made, she said, and this conjured to my mind the thought of other days like this one when she must have made it for her P.J. and called him in from outside for it. While she went to the kitchen I looked at the floor, not wanting further to embarrass the poor little room and the memory of the poor, friendless boy who had lived there, and who was far more real to me now than he had ever been while he was alive.

Mrs. Jones watched me sip her lemonade with a look of longing, as if I might be her own lost boy come back to her. Without looking up, I said, "Mrs. Jones, Ma'am, I'm awful sorry about P.J. Everybody is." I looked up then to judge from her face how convincing I had been. I saw that she had taken for depth of feeling what was really my embarrassment over my hypocrisy.

"Thank you, hon'," she said. "Were you a friend of his at school?"

"Yes'm, we were in the same grade. I'm the one who bought his paper route from him. I hadn't finished paying for it. I still owe two dollars." I reached into my pocket and produced them. I rose and went toward her, holding them out.

In my fright, my uneasiness, I was on the verge of tears; the sight of the two dollar bills brought tears to Mrs. Jones's eyes, and hers made mine flow. She took me in her arms and we both cried. Mrs. Jones believed I was crying for her dead boy and for her; I was crying because I could not cry for him nor for her but only for myself. I, the best qualified person she could have found to pour out her grief to, the one who had been certified to have died the same death as her boy, was crying for myself, having just learned my first lesson in life's essential loneliness and of how the grieving heart grieves all alone, in unbridgeable isolation.

Now, just a little more than a year later, that lesson was being brought home to me. Only one person could have really comforted me now, one to whom the loss of my father would be the same as it was to me. That person did not exist and never would, now. This I knew because of information I had only recently acquired. It was to my father that I owed it.

ONE EVENING not many months past, my mother went out somewhere, leaving my father and me alone together in the house. She was still not back when bedtime came.

I was about to switch off my lamp when my father let himself into my room. He had something to tell me, he said.

I waited.

Something that would take a little while, he said.

I told him to go ahead.

It would be better, he said, if he told me in the dark, and he reached for the lamp switch.

I said I hoped it was not something that was going to make me sad.

No, but it might embarrass me.

I judged this to mean something that might embarrass him, for I could not think of anything he could say to embarrass me, and I encouraged him to go right ahead.

He switched off the lamp and lay down beside me. How much did I know about women? he asked.

It was one of the oddest, most flabbergasting questions ever put to me. What had come over my usually sensible father? I knew all there was to know about women. I had one for a mother, the same as everybody else. I had women teachers, women friends. I knew as many girls as I did boys. What was there about women to "know"?

Reproved for his silliness, my father let some time pass in silence. Then he said, "Do the girls sometimes say to you, or you to them, 'I'll show you mine if you'll show me yours'?"

I was scandalized.

"It's all right. You can tell me. I won't tell your mother."

Now I was offended at being disbelieved, and shocked at his suggestion that I share with him some

shameful secret to be kept from my mother. I did not
want to see any girl's—whatever they called it; and I
certainly did not want to show any girl mine. What
on earth for? What *had* come over my father? I just
wished my mother would come home right now and take
him off to bed with her and put a stop to this.

"Does your dingus sometimes swell up and get stiff?"

"No!" I cried.

"Not yet, eh? Well, it will before long now."

"Why? What's going to make it do that?"

"You're getting to be the age for it. It's nature. That's
why I asked if you'd ever seen a naked girl. If you had,
you would know—"

The only swellings I had experienced were painful
inflammations; one in that tender part sounded more
painful than any I had ever experienced. I interrupted
my father. "Isn't there anything I can do to keep it
from happening?" Then my mind played over to me
what he had just been saying that I was not attending
to: "—then once it's in, you go in and out, until—"
Horrors! Imagine exposing that sensitive part of me,
aggravated by swelling, to—Suddenly I realized that he
meant it swelled up like that not just once, but regularly, chronically.

I said, "You mean, it does that, swells up like that,
more than once? Often?"

"Hah! Boy, when you're young it's like that more
often than not. Just about every girl you see, or even
just think about, gets it up for you."

A terrible thought entered my mind. I began to suspect that either my father was lying to me, or else that
he had gone crazy.

Meanwhile he was continuing his lesson.

"You what?" I asked, although I really did not want to know.

"You spurt your stuff in her."

"What stuff? Not —?"

"No. It's a different stuff. Made in another part of you."

I had the sense of having become a stranger to this body of mine, which had kept so many of it secrets, guilty secrets, from me, which was soon to begin playing these dirty tricks on me.

"It just comes out the same place. It's your seed."

Something on the order of a watermelon seed was what I visualized.

"A fluid," he said.

Something on the order of pus was what I now visualized.

"And that," he concluded, "is how babies are made."

No wonder he had never given me the brother or sister I had asked for, if this was what you had to go through to make one! I felt horribly beholden to him for having made me.

"I'm never going to do that!" I declared.

My father laughed. "Oh, yes. You will," he said. "What's more, you'll like it too. Believe me."

Looking now at that man-shaped bandage, that human cocoon, I knew that my father would never make me the brother or sister for whom I longed now as never before.

VI

MUCH THAT WAS SAID during those next three days, in the corridors and on the grounds of the hospital, in the house in Clarksville at night, and in the cars travelling back and forth between the two places, passed over my head. Much that was meant to pass over my head did not. I wished it had.

I heard it said that in the condition he would be left in, if he lived, my father would be better off dead, and that he would sooner be. He had been the most active, the most restless of men, an outdoorsman who came in under a roof only to sleep, touchily independent, resentful of his stomach ailment and impatient almost to the point of ungratefulness with my mother's care of him. Life as an invalid, confined, helpless, attended upon by others, would be hateful—would be worse than death to him. And how would we support him? On whose charity would we live? Yet to say that I would sooner he died—not even to myself could I do it.

I heard that said more than once, and in the solemn nodding together of heads I saw it being said when I did not hear it. As time passed, the emphasis fell differently upon the words, altering their import. From worry that he might live and be a burden upon us and upon himself, it changed into a kind of relief that he was going to die.

Shunning company and seeking solitude all those three days, small and easily concealed, I overheard things never meant for my ears. My very invisibility exposed me to them. Just where I was, just when I heard one thing, or even whether it was spoken in a man's voice or a woman's, I cannot now remember. This vagueness, however, is not to be taken to mean that what I heard was trivial or quickly forgotten; on the contrary. The details have not faded from my memory—they were ob-literated instantly by the shock of dismay and pain and the rush of my resentment. Until then I had been inno-cently unhappy in the belief that my father was hurt while trying to get home from working late into the night, out on the road repairing a broken-down car, doing his poor best to support my mother and me. Sorrow enough. Guilt and obligation enough to carry through life—and so I would, so I have, never knowing but what that was the truth of the matter. But now I must forever wonder whether he had not instead been hurrying home from a night with another woman. Of him, it seemed, this could be suspected—indeed, almost taken for granted. I heard it said, and I could not gainsay it, for it explained as nothing else ever had those many lengthy and oddly strained visits of my mother's and mine to her parents or to her sister in Dallas. Having heard it, I would waver ever afterwards in my duty to my father's memory between loyalty, gratitude, regret almost too much to bear, and—never knowing but what I was being monstrously unfair to him—a feeling of betrayal amounting almost to hatred, especially when, in moments of bitterness and self-pity, I recalled all the pain and the privation that his death brought upon my mother and me.

YET THERE HAD BEEN THAT PISTOL in the house by then. Guns there had always been—sporting guns; now there was that man-killer. And there was that fiery, redheaded woman, murderously jealous-tempered—self-declared, self-proclaimed.

How naturally red my mother's hair was, I never knew; she touched it up regularly with henna. Just so, there came a time in our lives when I heard hot words, hissed so that I would not hear them, between my mother and father in the darkness, but no shot in the night was fired. She had me to think about. And by then she cared less than she had expected she would, than she once had.

We pretended to my grandmother and to my Aunt Gertrude that we had come to them just for a little vacation. My mother was always one to keep her troubles to herself. Especially this trouble. She did not want to be told that they had told her so. And I knew without her prompting me that on these visits I must be especially bright and chipper, heavy, sore and puzzled though my heart was.

They knew why we were there, and they told her that they had told her so. They had known from the start that it would come to this sooner or later. They had warned her before she married him that he was wild. Had been all his life. His own mother had given up on him. His father could do nothing with him. Bad blood. They had told her he could never be tamed—not knowing that they were only confirming her in her choice, that that streak of wildness was what attracted her to him. They had not known—she herself was just learning it, it was he who had shown it to her, had brought it out—that she was a pretty wild one herself.

She was not all that much older now—a few years only. How could so short a time have wrought so thorough a change? She was old before her time, my father told her. That was in response to her telling him it was time he acted his age.

It seemed that nothing he did could please her any more. Still in her twenties and already becoming conventional and stuffy, and toward him a scold and a nag. The fun and the excitement had all gone out of life, yet he was as ready for it as ever. She was the one who had changed. He had remained what he was when she took him, and she took him with both eyes open. She knew what she was getting. He had stayed true to himself; it was she who had misled him. Where had his hot-blooded, fun-loving, devil-may-care spitfire of a red-head gone? What had become of the adoring girl he had fought over that night at the dance in Lone Star? Where was she that other night, later, down on the square?

On summery Saturday evenings in Clarksville what you did was drive downtown and park on the square. You took a turn around and looked into all the store windows. Then, if you were a child, you joined the other children playing on the plaza around the monument. If you were a man, you joined the men on one of the corners for talk; you also, if you were a man, resorted from time to time to one of the alleys behind the square for a swig straight from the bottle. If you were a woman, you sat in your car and received visitors, and went and visited friends in theirs.

On one such evening I was playing on the plaza when a cry of "Fight!" was raised. Along with everyone else, I ran to watch. The fight was on the sidewalk directly in front of our car. One of the fighters was my father. This drew upon me the admiration and the envy of my playmates, and I basked in it, especially as he was plainly the one who was winning.

My father had returned to the car to find a man molesting his wife. He caught him leaning into the window and, between hiccups, breathing invitations to her in vapors of 90 proof. It was a good many years since he had had an opportunity to fight over her.

He was demonstrating that he had lost none of his prowess. He was sending the man reeling again and again with blows to the head, the heart, the midriff. Joe Goltz, the town night constable, now on the scene, stood by for a while, allowing my father a fitting amount of revenge for the insult to his honor he had suffered, then intervened. My father flung him aside and resumed his systematic and savage beating of the man. That drew a gasp of awe from my playmates which I appreciated.

Meanwhile, however, my mother was trying to look as if she were somewhere else. As if she were unaware of any disturbance. As if she were unacquainted with either contestant. I read her attitude (I should have known by then what it would be), and my pride in my father went sour. Oh, how tired she was of his showing off, making scenes! The little bully! How common! And at his age! Would he never grow up?

My father had been drinking himself, but he was not too drunk to see that his chivalry was going unappreciated, indeed, that it was despised by her to whom it was dedicated. It was his resentment over this that he was taking out on the drunken man. When the man could no longer stand up to be beaten, my father left him slumped on the sidewalk against a storefront. He drove us home in sullen silence.

When my mother and I got out of the car, he whipped it back out of the driveway and gunned off for a night on the town.

THERE WAS PRESENT AT THAT FIGHT on the square that night a person who had been absent from the one at the dance in Lone Star, and it was he who had made all the difference.

However, it was not my coming that had changed things. When I first came to know them, my parents seemed to me much younger, freer, more high-spirited than those of any child of my acquaintance. They were, in fact, younger than most of them, particularly my girl of a mother, but, in most cases, not by as much as they seemed to be. Yet even compared to their contemporaries, mine seemed livelier, more carefree, not to say reckless, more on the go, daring, full of fun, of laughter and song. My mother stopped singing, humming or whistling a tune only to sleep. She always had a joke for me. She was never too busy to make something for me or show me how something was done or to play games with me when illness or bad weather kept me indoors. She was always ready for my father's spur-of-the-moment, madcap suggestions. Life, when I was little, seemed a round of pleasures, of parties, excursions, entertainments, not always within the bounds of the law, always free from any sanctity on Sundays. And, of course, they must have had fun of kinds from which I was necessarily excluded —a supposition I base upon such things as that visit from Miss Lois, my teacher, their contemporary and friend, the night she lost all her clothes at strip poker.

She knew whom to come to in that state to have a nightcap with.

I was not, as a child, given that sense which I have seen in the faces and in the behavior of all too many children, that I was resented by either of my parents because my coming into their lives had spelled the end of their youth, had spoiled their fun with each other. I was welcomed. There was room in their small boat for me. The party went on. They gave me to feel that I made things all the merrier.

The truth was rather different from what it seemed to me. My coming had not only interrupted the fun, it had cast a pall over their lives. But this I was not to learn for years. If I was made to feel welcome, a part of the fun, it was in proportion to their relief that I was not, after all, going to be the burden and the tribulation I had at first promised to be. By the time my mind began registering and remembering, the pall had lifted, and, for my father at least, this was reason all the more to live for the day, with never a backward or a forward glance.

IT WAS MY STARTING SCHOOL that changed our lives— not just mine, but my parents' as well. The unforeseen consequences of that seemingly commonplace step! From this perspective of years, I can see that the clash of wills that arose, and steadily sharpened, between my parents, and brought about the deterioration of their once-happy marriage, my father's drunkenness, illness, infidelity and, just possibly, his death, all had their beginning on that September day in 1930 when I enrolled in first grade in Clarksville's grammar school.

At school I met children from that neighborhood which we had never been able to afford to live in. My quickness as a pupil and my presentability made friends for me among them. They invited me to their houses to play with them after school and on Saturdays. My mother saw to it that I went neatly dressed and well drilled on my manners. My new friends' mothers were favorably impressed with me and I was asked to come again. I was invited to their birthday parties and they to mine. I got to know the Marable boys, the Dinwiddie boys, the Spencer boys, the Wren boys. I made close friends with John Thomas Felts, descendant of that Captain Clark who was Clarksville's founder.

All this went to my mother's head. Instead of the lifelong burden upon her that he was at first expected to be, this bright, well-behaved, outgoing little boy of hers, as nimble as any and more clever than most, whom all the world seemed to like, might be the key to doors she had never expected to see the inside of. He might be the first of all his kind ever to go to college, earn a living by his wits instead of with his hands. The sudden change, the almost overnight worsening of the times, coinciding with my starting school, had frightened and sobered her. It was imperative that I make my way into a sphere of life where living was not the tricky balancing act it was for us.

So, herself my tailor, my mother dressed me better than my betters, and upon my narrow shoulders she laid an obligation to be the brightest boy in my class. She then set to work to reform my father. He needed a general overhaul. It was time he shaped up and settled down, quit drinking, kept less disreputable company, bridled that temper of his and stopped making scenes in public.

WHILE IT DID NOT TURN HIS HEAD as it did my mother's, it pleased my father, too, to have a child who was bright, studious and promising. To see that I got the chance to fulfill my promise he was prepared to make a sacrifice. He was willing to keep me in school for as far as I was able to go, not take me out and put me to work to earn my keep, lighten his load. He hoped I might go on and become a lawyer, which to him was to play the smartest of all tricks on the world, to earn a living without working for it, to twist the law without breaking it, become a prime rascal, and wind up living in a big house on Silk Stocking Street staffed by servants, like Lawyer "Red" Robbins.

However, my father certainly saw no need for him to change any of his habits, pleasures, associations or anything else in order to advance me. He could not have changed if he had wanted to. Nobody would have believed in his reformation if he had sprouted wings. He had gained a certain reputation; given another lifetime to do it in, he could not have lived it down. He was what he was, take him or leave him.

My father knew just where he stood with the people of his town. He knew how the sort whose acceptance my mother now aimed for felt about him. He serviced their cars.

He had been born an outsider and he would always be one, socially a piney-woods pore-white, personally a rebel and a loner. Oh, he was well enough liked. Not a white man in the county called him "Mister"; he was "Clarence" or "Shorty" or " 'Ump" to all. But though he was everybody's friend, he was nobody's good friend. He was the sort of fellow who would be given the biggest funeral in the town's history, but who would never be invited inside the mourners' houses as long as he lived.

Independent, touchy, contrary, he balked at my mother's campaign to reform him—and when my father balked, he was a mule; the more you pushed and tugged him, the more stubbornly he stood his ground.

He had been through all this before, with his own mother. It was what had delayed him for so long, made him so careful in choosing a wife. It was what he thought he was getting away from in choosing my mother. That she was a free—which was to say, a lawless—spirit like himself. He was too old to be told now how to behave, what friends to have, when and with whom and how much to drink. He was his own man. He was not to be ordered around.

And why did this have to come just now? For it was not just my mother's efforts to reform him so that he would be a credit to his son that drove my father to drink, drove him out of the house, drove him eventually into other women's arms. It was not nearly so simple as that. It was a combination of things. It was his mounting, steady, sullen rage against the forces affecting him, things he could not comprehend, hardship that he had done nothing to bring about. He had never benefitted from the stock market boom; why should he suffer now in the bust? It was his betrayal by a system that promised reward to a man who did honorable, honest, hard work, and now was reneging on its promise. It was the deepening strife with his business partner. To all these things, the change in my mother and her attempts to change him were an added irritation, and an additional bewilderment. Here he was, beset by enemies and worries on every side, and his only ally against them, his sole refuge and comfort, his wife, seemed to have gone over to their side.

THE STOCK MARKET CRASH, and even the depression that followed it, seemed at first remote from us. Few people in our part of the country had ever seen a stock certificate. We had no money to invest in anything. We were content to earn enough to live on and put a little away for the time when we could no longer earn our living. To us, "Wall Street" stood for a few rich speculators, mostly Yankees, who had now overreached themselves. So let them find jobs and learn how the rest of us lived. Some businesses slowed and men were laid off work— men in Northern mills and factories, not farmers and tradespeople like us. Of more concern to us was this dry spell we were in.

It was not our seared lawns that bothered us nor the early shedding of the leaves from the trees, which had made our streets shadeless already by midsummer; it was the farmers' plight we worried over, for their plight was ours. The cotton was straggly and stunted. This year's corn looked like last year's cornstalks left standing in the fields over the winter. Stockponds had shrunk, the dried mud of their beds peeling and curling like old weathered housepaint. People were hauling water. The sun rose early and set late and never a cloud appeared in the sky. Fissures opened in the hard-baked earth.

The time was long past when Clarksville had styled

itself "The long-staple cotton capital of the world," but cotton was still King. We were the last demesne of cotton's kingdom. It had moved westward from the eastern seaboard in each generation. Cotton is destructive to the soil. The way farmers treated the land in those times, most any crop was destructive to the soil, but cotton is a plant that takes all and returns nothing. This had not mattered then; there was always new land, farther west. Let those left behind replenish the soil, rotate their crops. It was in cotton. that a man might make a sudden fortune.

This pernicious notion—for cotton was never a money-maker for the yeoman farmer—received new stimulation when, just after the First World War, cotton soared to forty cents a pound. Even Will Humphrey had cleared money that year. There was a regular cotton fever then, with still more land planted to it. Never mind that in the fifteen years since then cotton had gone back to twelve, ten, eight cents a pound; it had once reached forty cents a pound—was a man going to be the one fool not to plant it when there was always the chance that it might do that again?

Now there was no more west to go to; westward lay land suitable only for grazing. So our people grew cotton, and all of us depended on that crop. We were about to reap the whirlwind.

When the crop failed that fall it meant, to us, that my father would have to wait a whole year to be paid what he was owed by many of his customers. Not only those who made their living directly from cotton, but those who supplied them.

There was scant rainfall that winter. By time for spring planting the land was already parched. Farmers broke it, planted it with seed bought on credit, and waited for rain. Weeks passed and no rain fell. Then enough rain fell to germinate the seed and sprout the seedlings. Then there was no more rain and the seedlings wilted. In the recently plowed ground the fissures reopened; in unplowed ground those left open from last year widened and deepened. The earth looked like a jigsaw puzzle that had been put together and then jarred apart. One had to learn to walk on the detached pieces of earth as on stones in a creek. Once that summer, playing in my own back yard, I fell into a crack so deep I had to yell for my mother to come from the house and pull me out.

A wind sprang up. The wind always blew hard over our level land—this one did not blow itself out, it blew incessantly. It gathered up the powdery, rootless earth and a new weather phenomenon was born: the dust storm. A pall hung over us. Seen through this pall, the swollen sun was like some throbbing and feverish inflammation.

Wells went dry. The country people straggled into town like wanderers in the desert to an oasis. From deep in the country, from deep in the pinewoods they came— lost tribes: hermitlike, *farouche* creatures afraid of us townspeople but dependent now upon our meager hospitality. Gaunt, parched-looking, with hollow, pained, puzzled eyes, apologetic over their failure and their dependency now upon charity. Believers, like Job's comforters, in the doctrine that the wicked are punished not in the hereafter but in this life, and, thus, that the punished are wicked, their look was guilty and hangdog. The people of Clarksville took them in, shared them out. Though we had retrenched even our modest style of living and were then sharing a small duplex house on Washington Street, we took in a family of four. The man tried to make himself useful around my father's shop, the woman helped my mother around the house, the children spent their time watching me from a distance and running to hide if I so much as turned to look at them. They stayed with us several weeks, then found a ride with others like themselves going west—one of that gathering horde of our people going forth, ill-equipped and low in spirit, to make a new life for themselves in that promised land which was to receive them so inhospitably.

WHEN *Barton & Humphrey* BROKE UP, the ex-partners divided the assets of the firm; that is to say, each took half of the unpaid bills owing to it. On the eve of the first of the month, my mother copied them all and mailed them out. In the beginning, she was incensed, determined to have what was ours, every last cent of it. These bills represented her husband's labor: skilled, honest, hard labor—not to mention the replacement parts, which in each case accounted for most of the bill, that he had paid for out of his own pocket.

The eve of the next month, and the next, and the next found her copying and sending out the same bills again. The anger welled, then slowly ebbed out of her. She had been living in these bad times long enough to see for herself that most of our debtors were truly unable to pay what they owed us. She went on dutifully copying and mailing out the bills; but now it was weariness and futility that filled her, pity for her man and for his lost, hard work.

Once, out of some perverse prompting for self-torment, she added them all up. They totalled just under ten thousand dollars—an immense sum of money to her. She would have been frightened to possess such a sum of money; to be owed it and be unable to collect it was heartbreaking. For a man whose ambition was to earn a steady hundred dollars a month, it was a huge amount of labor lost. This was like being told by a doctor that he had some dread disease. Should she or should she not tell him? It was too terrible to bear alone; she told him.

He had not known it was as much as that. The figure stunned him.

He looked through the bills. Some of them were now four, five years overdue. He picked out one. "This man hasn't even owned his car for the past six months," he said. "The finance company repossessed it for non-payment. He doesn't own any car. Poor devil is on foot now." Another one made him say, "I can't ask this man for money. He can barely keep his family decently clothed." He picked out another. "Now here," he said, "is somebody who could pay. He will be the last one we'll ever see a nickel from."

He looked through more of them, shaking his head whenever one recalled to him some particularly difficult and expensive job, the skinned knuckles it had cost him, the visit to the eye doctor to remove the splinter of steel from the grinding wheel.

"Don't waste any more of your time, Nell," he said. "Don't throw away good money on any more postage stamps. These people all know what they owe me. Reminding them of it won't do any good. The honest ones among them will pay me if they ever can. The others never will, and no amount of dunning will make them."

He could stand the sight of them no longer. He swept them into a paper bag and, in the back yard, he made a bonfire of them, wadding each one into a ball before tossing it into the flames. In a few minutes all record of the work of years lay in ashes.

IN TIMES LIKE THESE was it any wonder if a man took an occasional drink, even an occasional drink too many? If, waiting around the shop for work that never came, or doing a job which he knew beforehand he was not going to get paid for, he felt, at the end of the day, like letting off a little steam? Waiting in this heat for rain that never came, a man got hot and thirsty, and the fuse of his temper grew short.

A sullen resentment burned steadily in him, unbroken as the drought, persistent as this depression. Literally, it gnawed at him. His ulcer worsened, the pain grew constant. His pleasure in eating was taken from him. Once he had blackened his plate with pepper, doused it with chili sauce; now even unseasoned food disagreed with him. The medicine chests at home and at the shop swelled with nostrums for heartburn, acid indigestion, dyspepsia. He consulted a doctor. Told by the doctor to quit drinking, he changed doctors and drank all the harder.

Cars were faster than ever and he drove them all the faster. My mother would plead with him to slow down. He would set his jaw and press the accelerator to the floorboard. He hated nothing so much as a backseat driver. She demanded that he quit drinking; he came home reeling drunk, or he did not come home at all. She reproached him for staying out. That was what he was staying away from: a home in which he got reproaches. As if he did not have troubles enough—a wife who had turned shrewish on him.

Now there were many meals in our house when discord, silent but oppressive, had a place at our table like an uninvited guest. There were periods when it seemed to have become a regular boarder with us. When it seemed to have replaced my father as the man in our family, when it sat at his place at the table with my mother and me. There were periods when I seldom saw him. Already gone off to work when I was served my breakfast, he was still not home when I was put to bed.

My father's absences from home in the evenings ended by driving me onto the street as well. Many were the nights I played late—joylessly but late—under the streetlamps because I did not want to go home to my unhappy house. Many were the evenings my mother spent alone. Many an evening I was still nervously awake when my father came home, and I buried my head beneath my pillow so as not to hear their angry voices.

I took no side. I put the blame for things on neither the one nor the other of them. There was no blame to assign. I just wanted them to declare an armistice, make up, get along together. I wanted things to be as they had been before.

THE TIMES had given rise to a wave of crime—in the cities of the North, organized crime, gangs; among us, more individual, more rural crime, with a new twist to it, but with roots in old traditions of ours.

The Southerner, and even more the Texan, was always gun-ready. A lawsuit could not satisfy his injured honor; he must avenge himself personally, man to man. With his home-grown outlaws he always felt a certain sympathy. His heroes were Jesse James, Sam Bass, and, later, Pretty Boy Floyd, Clyde Barrow and Bonnie Parker: robbers of those banks which had foreclosed on his mortgage, closed down on his deposit. The Texan was descended from, and at that date not long removed from, some Southerner for whom even the wide latitude of tolerance for his quick temper and his wayward ways back home was too narrow, and who had "G.T.T."—Gone to Texas, the understanding being that he had gone just one step ahead of the law. At that date he still had living, or not long dead, a grandaddy or two who had taken up arms and fought against the government of the country. Had fought and lost despite waging the nobler fight, and had festered ever afterwards in his wounded pride and looked upon that government as alien, imposed upon him by his conquerors, by lawmakers not of his choosing, far away and indifferent to him when not actually bent upon his subjugation and exploitation, in whose decisions his only say was the maneuvers of his parliamentarians, men skilled in the delay of government, token members only of their parliament in any case.

Now, dispossessed and driven off their land and turned adrift in cities where there was no use for their country crafts, nothing but contempt for their country ways, such men turned truculent and resentful, vengeful, and the lawlessness and violence just beneath their skin erupted. The sense of helplessness, of the futility of trying to get ahead through hard work when there was no work to be had, turned desperate men into desperadoes, and a sympathetic public followed their exploits in the papers and secretly cheered them on.

New uses were found for that still new but already fixed feature of life, the automobile. They could be stolen, they could be used to get away from holdups, bank robberies, highjackings. They could be used to transport liquor—now legally flowing again elsewhere— into areas, like ours, that were still dry through local option. There was no end to the possibilities for mobile mischief that had newly opened up.

It was the crime wave that brought the pistol into our house. In this age of Public Enemies we lived in their very midst, in their very breeding ground. Pretty Boy Floyd and Clyde Barrow and Bonnie Parker: to us they were practically the kids next door. We ourselves knew people who had known them when they were growing up. Hereabouts, nowadays, no man's life was safe; a man involved with cars was constantly exposed to danger. These highwaymen stole cars continually, and as often as not they left the owner dead. Garages and filling stations were favorite targets of theirs. My father was often out on the road late at night, alone, far from help. The chance that he would ever need the pistol was one in a million, but having it made him feel safer.

To me that one in a million chance was enough for the pistol to add a good foot to my father's stature— and as much to my own, as well. What other boy had a father who carried a pistol in a quick-draw shoulder holster just like the men in the movies did? I could not understand why I was told by both my parents, separately, not to tell anybody about it.

In no time at all my father was a crack pistol-shot. He could whip it from its holster and empty it into the exact same spot time after time. Despite my mother's objections, he taught me to shoot it—or tried to. I shut my eyes and flinched and imagined I was killing somebody each time it roared and bucked in my hand.

Ordinarily my mother had no fear of guns—not in my father's hands. And so long as I was in his hands, she had no fear of my handling guns, not even when I was only four years old, my age when he bought me a 22-caliber repeating rifle and taught me to shoot it. By the time I was ten, she trusted me off alone with it; that was the measure of her confidence in the training my father had given me, and her freedom from fear of firearms in themselves. But the pistol was different.

If I had expected the pistol to put an end to the quarrelling in our house by renewing my mother's admiration for my father, I was disappointed—and thereby a little disappointed in her. I looked at the pistol, and at him, with eyes wide with wonder, but she looked at both askance, with eyes narrowed by—by I did not know what.

It was as if my father had brought home with him, without telling my mother to expect it, some new companion he had picked up somewhere—somewhere of which she would not have approved—one who brought out the worst in him. She said nothing against it. She carefully refrained, as though it had ears and might revenge itself upon her if she should. Her disapproval was confined to the way she looked at it, and at him whenever he strapped it on before leaving the house.

I could see that my mother was skeptical of the reason my father gave for acquiring his pistol. She did not trust him with it, especially in the mood he was in those days: angry all the time at everything, bitter and resentful, a man with as many grievances, real and fancied, as there were cartridges in the magazine of that gun. She wondered what he was planning—doing—what he had done to make him feel the need of that thing.

The papers I delivered each afternoon were filled with stories of holdups and getaways, shoot-outs and ambuscades. The life stories of the bandits: how fearfully close they were to people I myself knew. Knew? Was related to. My father's brother: a poor boy fresh off the farm, unable to get work in town, falls in with bad company, is led astray, commits a crime, winds up in jail. I went to the movies and, totally, terrifyingly convinced, watched James Cagney, in just ninety minutes, go wrong and come to a bloody end. It was almost like seeing him in the flesh as I watched my father practice and become deadly with that pistol, watched him at the wheel of our car always as if someone were hot in pursuit of him. I suspected my father of nothing, but I could not help wondering about him, and if I did, he had only himself to blame.

Now I must wonder whether there had not been yet another threat hanging over my father. After overhearing that conjecture about where he was coming from on the night he got hurt, there would be added to the cast of characters in that other life he led away from home the shadowy figure of some violent-tempered husband, jealous and with reason to be suspicious of his wife's fidelity.

To GET TO THE HOSPITAL in the morning, and again coming back to Clarksville in the evening, we drove through Mabry. There, for a short period, only recently ended, my parents and I had led an entirely different sort of life for us, one that, while it lasted, restored some of our old, lost happiness together.

My father still carried his pistol, and I still wondered and speculated why. He still suffered from his ulcer, though less. Terrible as it was to have to admit it, the ulcer was the thing to which we owed the peace that had been restored among us. It had slowed him down. His diet was still restricted, my mother's artistry in the kitchen sharply limited. Now after lunch he had to lie down for an hour's rest, and I must keep quiet or else go off out of hearing. We stayed much at home. There was no reviving the gaiety, the restless round of fun of our early years together. But my father had, perforce, quit drinking. There were no more fights. The fight had gone out of them along with the fun. But at least he came home from work at night—unless work kept him late. At least my mother and I did not go off periodically to stay with her sister Gertrude in Dallas. She and I had, together, an engrossing new interest.

Mabry was a hamlet of a dozen or so houses, a few along the highway, a few others down the dirt road leading off it, a church and a graveyard near where the two roads met. Ours, which we rented, was one of the houses on the dirt road, a newly built little cottage surrounded by five acres of its own. It was the first time we had ever lived in the country. It was spring; school was just out. It was like being on vacation with no end to it in sight.

The cottage was so tiny that living in it was like playing house, and the sense this gave of make-believe heightened the pleasure my mother and I took in it. We did not feel cramped, we felt snug. For us it was like the cottage in a fairy tale.

My mother became a girl again—that is to say, she became the girl that, because of the injury to her hand, she never had been: a country girl. She who had been spared all such work on the farm, and who had been determined never to do it, laid out a kitchen garden. A neighboring farmer broke the sod and plowed the ground; together my mother and I fenced in our plot. We staked out the rows, planted the seeds, and labelled the rows with the empty seed packets. Before anything was above ground, we made, out of a worn suit of my father's coveralls, a scarecrow to protect our crop.

Early each morning we inspected our garden for signs of germination. When the first seedlings appeared, we were as proud as though we were the first ever to preside over such an event. Each morning we measured their overnight growth. Farm girl though she had been, it was the first time in her life that my mother had experienced the satisfaction of growing something with her own hands. Town boy that I was, it was my first time, too. Spurred by our success with vegetables, we planted flowerbeds.

"I'll tell you what let's do!" said my mother one day. "Let's raise us some chickens! We'll have our own pullets, fryers, our very own country-fresh eggs!"

"But we haven't got a chicken house."

"We don't need a very big one. A dozen layers will give us all the eggs we can use."

"But we haven't got even a little one."

"Let's build one!"

"Who?"

"You and me!"

"Do you think we could, Mother?"

"Sure we can! What's to stop us?"

The house, as I said, was newly built. Still on the site, left over from the building, was a sizeable quantity of lumber. It was this my mother had her eye on. She now asked the owner if she could have it. She told him what she had in mind, and pointed out to him that a chicken house would enhance the value of his property. I did not hear her specify who the builders were to be. I was not at all sure that any construction in which I had a hand would be an addition to the place. I could see that my mother's enthusiasm was running higher all the while, and I hated to dampen it, but there was something she was forgetting and which she ought to be warned about.

"Mother," I said, "you remember when we were living in Texarkana?"

"Mmh?"

We had lived in Texarkana—a miserable time for me—for several months the previous year. The partnership between my father and Mr. Barton had dissolved, and we had gone to Texarkana where my father got a job as foreman in a big garage. He wanted to learn there the latest techniques in car repair, the latest tools.

"Well, you remember that class I took in woodworking?"

That course, required of all boys, in what was called "Shop," had been one of the main causes of my misery in Texarkana. You were given a semester in which to produce (1) a breadboard, (2) a tie rack, and (3) a hanging corner whatnot shelf. By the end of the semester I had ruined four pieces of wood and still had not succeeded in producing a square, level breadboard. The teacher had never before encountered such unteachable ineptitude.

"Never mind that," said my mother. "I'll show you what to do. It'll come to me because it's in my blood. I'm not an old country girl for nothing."

Sure enough, things she did not know she knew came to her. She delighted in herself. "Now where did I ever pick up that trick, do you suppose?" she would say, using the spirit level to plumb up a stud, or squaring a board and sawing off the end straight and true. She tried the board, fitting it in place. It measured right. "You know, when you *have* to do something, you *do* it." She selected a nail from one of the pockets of her apron and started it. "If you and me were to be stranded on a desert island, we'd get by. It all comes from being brought up on a farm. Farmers have to know a little bit of everything. There!" driving the nail home with that good left hand of hers and humming a snatch of tune, "Not many Clarksville dames of your acquaintance can do that, Mister!"

Adjustments, which is to say, enlargements, in our original plans were made as we went along. As my mother observed, as long as you were building a chicken house, it was only sensible to build a decent-sized one. It was no more work to cut a long plank than to cut a short one; in fact, it was less. And as long as the lumber was there, and didn't cost you anything . . . So the dozen layers grew into two dozen. The extra eggs we would sell. With that money we would buy chicken feed. Our own eggs would cost us practically nothing.

"What do you think of that, hey?" my mother would demand of my father when she brought him to inspect the construction site. "Didn't think your little old lady was up to anything like that, I bet, did you? Look as close as you like. Go ahead. Take a plumb line to it. Take the tape measure. Take the spirit level."

We watched our creation rise, day by day, and our self-satisfaction rose with it. We had a right to be proud: thirty-two years later our chicken house would be still standing and in use. When it was finished, roofed and painted, we had roosts, nesting boxes, feed troughs, storage bins, a door with a latch, a pen, wire-netted to keep out chicken hawks. We had everything but the chickens. Before we could get those, the owner of the house was suddenly obliged to put it up for sale. My mother longed with all her heart to buy it. She wanted never to move back into town. But we did not have the four hundred dollars asking price. Someone else bought the house, we were given notice, and, without ever harvesting our garden, we moved back to Clarksville, into the apartment where we were living when, just weeks later, my father got killed.

VII

THE HOUSE WAS FULL OF WHISPERS, hurried whispers. Already plans were being made for our future, in haste, for there was nothing to buy time with. Even before my father's body was in the ground, negotiations were under way with his new business partner for the sale of his mechanic's tools—now, following the destruction of the car, a total loss, the most valuable thing he had left behind him, worth a couple of hundred dollars. His life had been insured for a thousand dollars. Out of this his funeral expenses and all our debts would have to be paid.

It went without saying that my mother and I would have to move away, for there was no way for her to earn us a living in Clarksville. There the only working women were schoolteachers, doctors' nurses (usually the doctor's wife), storekeepers. My mother was not trained for anything, lacked the money to open a store. She had sometimes worked on Saturdays as a salesclerk in Silberberg's Dry Goods Store on the square, during the fall when the crops were in and the farmers in town with money to spend. Her hours were from seven in the morning until ten at night. She was paid one dollar. Aside from this the only things she knew how to do were sew, cook and keep house. She was good at all three, but in Clarksville all women sewed for themselves, while the cooking and housework, if hired, were done by colored women. A white woman, and her fatherless children, would have been allowed to starve before she was offered domestic work, and would have starved herself and her children before she would have accepted it.

New trees grow in soil enriched by fallen older trees. In that same native soil that had been my father's, and to which he was now returning, nurtured on him, I might have grown straight—never tall, but straight.

Now, still spindly, my taproot all that I had put out and
it still stubbornly rooted in the soil of Clarksville, I was
to be plucked up and transplanted. Wild plants take
poorly to city soil. Many grow stunted, wither, droop and
die. That I would be one of that kind seemed certain
to me.

We would be going to Dallas, where my mother
might hope to find some kind of work, where one of her
sisters would take us in, poor and cramped for space
though she and her family were already. Dallas: that
vastness of tall buildings, endless suburbs, concrete and
asphalt. My days afield and in the woods, my hunting
days were over. I would never be the wingshot my father
had hoped to make of me. I had lived for short periods in
other places: Austin and Texarkana, both smaller and
less terrifying than Dallas, and I had been a fish out of
water, gasping for my native element with my every
breath. To think of leaving it forever, the square, the
familiar streets, the familiar faces, the people I had
known all my life, had grown up with, and going
among strangers—this was as painful to me then as
the death of my father was. Once I had been brought
back to life from drowning; at the prospect of being
thrown to sink or swim in Dallas, I felt exactly as though
I were about to drown again. My old talisman, my death
certificate, even if I had had it still, would do me no
good now. Indeed, the me that I knew lay with my father
in his coffin, would shortly be buried with him in his
grave. In Clarksville a child sometimes met people whom
he did not know, but not people who did not know him.
"Oh, you're Clarence Humphrey's boy," they said to me.
If they did not, then I said it to them. That was who I
was: Clarence Humphrey's boy. Not any more. In my

mind already I could hear strange, faceless Dallas boys ask me what my father did. "He's dead," I heard myself reply. Then they would be embarrassed, and not know what to say. That was what I had become: an embarrassment.

WE WERE NOT AT HOME. We had not been back there since leaving it early on Monday morning. Now, with the loss of my father, we had ceased to have a home. We were in my mother's parents' house. Not out in the country at their old farmhouse; that they had been forced to leave when the last of their twelve children left home. They had moved into town, where my grandfather found what work he could as a carpenter. They now rented a house on Third Street—the one directly across from the charred foundation on which our house that burned had stood. It was in this house that my mother and I were put up and looked after while my father was in the hospital and at the undertaker's.

Early on the first morning of my father's death, at the hour when work was commencing on his body to ready it for burial, Third Street sent its men, with their lunchpails, quietly off to their work, then for the rest of the day muffled itself in a silence that converted it into something resembling a hospital corridor. Window-shades were not raised, doors not slammed, radios not turned on. Morning lengthened: a bright, hot, out-of-school, midsummer morning—and still the children, once my playmates, were not let out to play, or else were told to play by themselves in their own back yards, quietly and out of sight. The housewives did not appear on their porches to shake out mops, dustcloths. Peddlers were turned back at the ends of the street that day. Out of consideration for the trouble in our house, the neighborhood was edged in black and normal life suspended, as when a funeral procession rolled through the square downtown and commerce and sociability were interrupted while men bared their heads and women lowered their gaze.

And yet, as I had witnessed—been a part of—once the procession had passed through the square, life was resumed, went on as before. The town clock never missed a chime.

And, just as I could now easily imagine that not every woman in a funeral procession was wholeheartedly absorbed in grief, but might, behind her veil, be going over in her mind some old quarrel with the deceased that had never stopped rankling, or wondering whether the slight indisposition that she herself had felt for the past several days might not be the warning symptom of the very malady to which her late friend had succumbed, or just rehearsing the guest list for her coming dinner party, so I could imagine that behind their drawn shades the housewives of Third Street were going about their lives with nothing more heartfelt than a sigh for us, glad that the rules of propriety gave them an excuse for quarantining us and shutting out of their homes the unpleasantness which we had brought into their midst, that no doubt they were drawing a cautionary and comforting moral from our misfortune, and congratulating themselves on its having happened to us and not to them. If this was so, then I did not blame them. Had I been in their place and they in mine, I would have felt that way too. But it saddened me that I could now attribute such ulterior motives to my former neighbors and friends, for it was another indication of the premature wisdom, or, at least, the suspiciousness, the mistrust, which, like some hand-me-down suit of clothes far too big for me and too grown-up in style, but which I must grow into, I had put on in these past few days.

The daily rides to Paris—trips to the torture chamber—the vigil on the hospital grounds, the summonses to my father's bedside, each more dreadful, more hopeless than the last: the anguish which had driven all else out of my mind and reduced me to a mindless mass of pain—all that was over now. My tormentors had given me this day off, to convalesce, to regain my senses, so as to feel to the full tomorrow's ordeal: the funeral.

And then? Then people would put their hats back on and take off their veils and resume their lives where they had interrupted them, and shortly my father would no more be missed from among the multitudes of men than a single fallen star, the moment it is gone, can be missed from among the millions still shining in the sky. To me alone had he been a father. To me alone was he irreplaceable, the sun of my little universe.

The room that my mother and I had been put in looked out on the street, with a view of that blackened foundation across the way. There I had secluded myself, and, deaf to all efforts to coax me out, sat staring out the window. My behavior, strange from the start, was becoming worrisome.

Throughout all that had happened during these past three days, I, whom it touched the most deeply, who had been exposed to it all at its grisliest, its most rending, had not been moved to shed a tear—the only person involved in any way who had not. Even my cousins of my own self-concerned and shallow age had. The very nurses at the hospital had. Even those two stones, those two fenceposts, my emotionally deficient grandfathers, had. The women had hardly stopped. Inside the house now, where all talk was muted, all coming and going on tiptoe, the murmur of their weeping was as incessant as the flow of a brook. Only I remained as dry-eyed as a basilisk. I wondered at myself—what then must they be thinking of me? That I was an abnormality, a selfish, unfeeling, heartless little monster whose love for his father had been feigned, produced just for what he could get out of him?

No. When I shunned the women's attempts to hug me to their heaving bosoms, they thought I was suffering too much to cry and that what I needed, like a purgative when a child's digestion was blocked, was a good dose of tears. When I greeted in sullen silence my uncles' commendations on being a brave little man, they thought I was struggling manfully not to show my suffering, in the belief that this was expected of me now that I had turned thirteen, now that I was the man in my family.

I could not explain my behavior to myself, and I was made to feel that it needed explanation. It was one of the many things I was discovering about myself that set me apart and made me feel different, peculiar, and lonely. Instead of seeking company and comfort in my unhappiness, I wanted only to be left alone. I could not bear what the sight of me did to people. My mother, for example, would be holding up fairly well; I would hear her talking with people on distracting topics and without any catch in her voice—but at the sight of me she melted. In every eye I looked into I saw a new reflection of myself, one as unrecognizable but just as undeniable as my father's battered body had been. I was pitied— I who had always thought of myself as lucky, even envied. The sight of me made grown people turn away and cry. Especially, of course, my grown relatives. And I could see—as I could now see in other people lots of things I had never seen before—that they feared me, too. I had become a poor relation, a dependent—one whom, in their own straitened circumstances, they could not afford to assume. This made them ashamed of themselves, and thus resentful of me, the cause of their shame.

My cousins looked at me from a distance, curiously and with fear, as though my bad luck might be catching if they came too close, and their looks made me say to myself over and over, "I haven't got a daddy any more." What made me still stranger to myself was that I was only the second boy I had ever known who did not have one. I resented mine for dying. I resented his recklessness, his irresponsibility, which had left me fatherless, unprotected and poor. I was ashamed of being fatherless, different from—which to a child means, inferior to —children with fathers.

AENEAS, when he was driven from his home town, went carrying his father on his back. So did I, so do we all, whether bodily or in memory, and the burden is as heavy either way. But, like Aeneas after the burning of Troy, I would be carrying little else. In going to Dallas, my mother and I would be travelling light. So we had been doing—the three of us, that is—even in our moves around Clarksville over the past few years. Indeed, we had never been very heavily encumbered with goods, even in our fattest times. It had never been the work of more than a couple of days for my mother to pack us for the moving van. Staring now at that charred foundation across the street, I was struck by how small a cinerarium sufficed to hold the ashes of our years' accumulation. From that crippling blow to our always frail finances, we had never fully recovered. Many of the things we had lost, we had never been able to replace.

Had I gone across the street and raked among those ashes, no doubt I would have turned up things that had come through the fire retaining enough of their original shape to be identifiable. If so, they would have been things in common use, made from basic, coarse materials like iron, clay, fire-resistant because they had been through the fire before, in getting made, and had come out of it vitrified, hardened, tempered. The formless and indistinguishable ashes would be the residue of things perishable from the start, trinkets and trivia, enjoyed once and then put away in the vain but inextinguishable human hope of preserving and rediscovering past pleasures in keepsakes, snapshots, souvenirs— inanimate objects which, deprived of their myriad original associations (which is to say, their ephemerality), bear no more resemblance to the moments they are meant to memorialize than dead butterflies pinned on a card do to living ones. Just so with that bed of ashes that now constituted my memories: those that had come through had been born in fire, those of lighter stuff had all gone up in smoke. My durable memories were those that, being made of life's basic sadness, were exchangeable with others; those that had burned were personal to me.

Was it that my present suffering had blinded me to the times when I was happy; or—since it had left me dry-eyed—had it cleared my sight and shown me that there never was a time when I had been? Was it just my nearness to that charred foundation that, for the moment, seemed to have reduced my whole life up to now to ashes? Certainly it was true that of no other house of all the many I had lived in did I retain so many unhappy memories. Was that not simply because it was the one in which I had lived the longest? But if that was so, why then was it not the one from which I had retained the greatest number of happy memories as well? Was it some affinity for gloom, some incapacity for balanced, wholesome-minded living that I was discovering in myself? Why had I torn the pages from my calendar and tossed them to the winds when they commemorated days that were free from care—what perversity, what morbidity of mind, what urge for self-torment had made me save in stacks the ones which, since I could never recall them, relive them, atone for them, were the very ones I would most have liked to forget? What had happened was that my happy memories, too precious for my handling, had been roped and sealed off even from me. I could see them, but, even to me, they had acquired a rarity, a strangeness and a patina, like things kept under glass, under lock and key, under guard. I could come and look, but, like any other visitor to the museum, I must not touch. The fact was, I had now advanced to that chapter in the textbook of life which teaches that pleasure is nothing but a short holiday from pain—or rather, that being the lesson from the first one on, I had begun at last to attend to what I was being taught.

THE FOURTH OF JULY was an unlucky time for me. On the eve of it, 1933, while my parents went down on the square, I was left to play outdoors with the children of our neighborhood. We gathered in the vacant lot cater-cornered across the street from the grammar school. Our game was "Tag." I was "It," and was chasing Sarah Goltz, with whom I had fallen in love that very evening, trying to tag her, when I slipped and fell and slid into a wooden stake hidden in the grass to which somebody's cow had been tethered by day. My right kneecap was sliced off. It hung by a tatter of skin. I felt no pain: the blow had numbed itself. There was only the faintest trickle of blood. A butcher separating at the joint a well-bled leg of lamb could not have done a neater job. While my playmates waited for me to get up and chase them, I sat staring at the empty socket where my knee had been. It was slick and shiny like the gristle of a soup-shank.

Grownups were summoned, I was laid on a back carseat, rushed downtown, my parents found, I was carried upstairs to one of those second-floor doctors' offices, laid on a table, my arms and legs pinned down, a kitchen sieve put over my nose and mouth, a cloth soaked in chloroform put over the sieve, I gagged, then went under. The image I took with me as I went was of my mother's tearful face.

It was a glorious day when I woke the next morning in my bed. The windows were open and a cool breeze blowing in. Birds sang in the tree just outside, the sycamore that my hobbyhorse hung from—my climbing tree. I heard in the distance the cries of children at play and the yapping of dogs. My leg was in splints and bandages, and when I asked with my first words how soon they would come off and I get up, my mother told me that I would have to spend the summer in bed.

A summer in bed! For me, to whom a house was a cage! No prisoner before a pitiless judge was ever given a more dismaying sentence. Summer: the season I lived all year for, getting through the other schoolridden and joyless ones like vegetables at supper in order to earn my dessert—and now it was snatched from me. In bed while the sun shone and the days were long—full when you were free, but endless when you were confined—and school was out and, long as they were, the days were never long enough to do all there was to do: swimming, picnicking, playing games, exploring. The frightening and pitiful image of Cleo Kelty strapped to her bedboard rose to my mind and I burst into tears, but it was not Cleo I was sorry for. My mother cried with me —cried harder than I did. She knew something she had not told me: that the doctor who performed the operation had said I would never bend that knee again.

My mother gave a party for me. All my schoolmates came, all with gifts for me of indoor amusements. My mother made my bed a playpen, and kept it piled with toys, puzzles, games. The radio was moved into my room. I listened to Stoopnagle and Bud, Fibber McGee and Molly, Singing Sam the Barbasol Man, Ma Perkins. And at night, after the lights were out, not being tired and sleepy, I listened through the earphones to the crystal set that James Storey had lent me—a magic carpet, a spaceship through the stars, which I could see through my window, transporting me to places halfway around the world.

James Storey came to see me after the party was over. It was like James to wait and let the crowds thin out before coming.

James lived just two doors away, but while he and I were friendly, we were not friends. His being three years older than I opened a gulf between us, this in addition to the gulf that divided James even from boys his own age. He was a very reserved boy—James to all, Jimmy to none: serious, solitary, delicate. Severe asthma kept him from all exertion and confined him much indoors, often in bed. I had played with him occasionally, but his mother did not much encourage my visits, no doubt fearing that I with my restlessness and excitability might overstimulate him and bring on one of his attacks. He, like me, was an only child. Around him and his unpredictable infirmity, his rather elderly parents regulated their lives.

Among the boys of town James was regarded as something of a wizard for his reading, his tinkering with scientific toys. These, and his books, he acquired by selling *Collier's* and *The American Magazine* out of a canvas satchel on the square. In addition to a commission on each copy, he earned vouchers which he redeemed for such things not to be bought in Clarksville as a miniature steam engine fuelled by alcohol, a telegraph key, battery-powered, new chemicals for his ever-expanding chemistry set. He subscribed to magazines, sent away for mail-order catalogues, wrote pen-pals. Housebound though he often was, James Storey was more in touch with the outside world than any other boy in town. He got more mail than any adult.

James was my opposite. I pouted and pined if kept indoors for a day; he was used to that. Without company, I just dried up, like a solitary drop of water; James was not only used to solitude, he made something out of it. James was a regular where I was now just a transient lodger. His evenness of temper, which perhaps he had had to learn in order to stave off his attacks, and his self-discipline, which gave him a maturity and an independence beyond his years, set an example for me now—an unattainable one, but an example. His sympathy for me was different from that of my other visitors —quieter and better-informed, and it made me feel less sorry for myself.

He came bringing me the first in the series of *Tom Swift* books, and the promise that as soon as I had finished it, I could borrow the next one from him. I was touched, grateful—even interested. Here was something I had not thought of to help me while away the time. But it was at best only a consolation; I was not overjoyed. I was no reader. Aside from textbooks, the only book I had ever looked into was a child's version of *The Arabian Nights*, given to me for Christmas when I was six. I had enjoyed it, but it had not stimulated me to read other books. Just as well, for Clarksville had no public library, nor was there one at school. No family that I knew owned a book.

James brought me something else that day that interested me more. Something to entertain me at night, even in the dark. Something money could not buy. This apparatus was mounted on a board. A cardboard cylin-

der, formerly a quart ice-cream container, wound closely
with copper wire as fine as hair, was fixed horizontally
on two posts. On a track running the length of the
cylinder, a thin, flexible needle moved across the wire;
a brighter line worn in the strands of copper showed its
path. Affixed to the board was a tiny lead cup molded
around the base of a quartz crystal. A needle which
could be moved to touch any facet of the crystal was
attached to a post beside it. Wires from all these parts
ran to a battery attached to the board and from the
battery to a pair of headphones such as telephone lines-
men wore. This was the crystal set radio, and James himself had made it. It was mine to keep now until I got
well, after which James would teach me how to make
one of my own. He would come again in the evening—
the reception was good only after dark—and show me
how to work it. He left—the sickly, considerate, courage-
ous boy who had just brought into my life the thing
which would one day help me more than anything else
to recuperate from a much worse wound than this:
books.

As she went about her housework, my mother
stopped singing a song only to start another one, or to
answer a knock at the door. *Just Molly and me; Come to
me, my melancholy baby; I wonder who's kissing her
now; A pretty girl is like a melody*: one drew forth another and she went through her whole medley, accompanied by the stirring of spoons in pots, the thump
of dough on the doughboard. From my bed I joined in
with her on the jaunty, carefree ones:

> *Oh, we ain't got plenty of money.*
> *It may be we're ragged and funny.*

But we'll travel along,
Singing a song,
Side by side.

I'm sitting on top of the world,
Rolling along,
Singing a song.
Just like Humpty-Dumpty,
I'm sitting on top of the wall;
Just like Humpty-Dumpty,
I'm going to fall.

In the mornin',
In the evenin',
Ain't we got fun!
Night and daytime,
Work and playtime,
Ain't we got fun!

She sang torch-songs to me as she straightened my room.

Sometimes I'm happy,
Sometimes I'm blue.
My disposition depends on you.
That's how I am, so what can I do?
I'm happy when I'm with you.

She made a dancing partner of her dry-mop and crooned to it as she mopped my floor. She sang:

You're the cream in my coffee,
You're the salt in my stew.

She sang:

Button up your overcoat, when the wind blows free.
Take good care of yourself—you belong to me.

Strumming on her imaginary strings and serenading as softly as a sea breeze, she transported me to isles of enchantment with:

> *If a-you like a-Ukulele Lady,*
> *Ukulele Lady like a-you.*
> *If a-you like a-linger where it's shady,*
> *Ukulele Lady linger, too.*

I would clap wildly as she pranced offstage to the words:

> *Ain't she sweet?*
> *See her coming down the street.*
> *I ask you very confidentially,*
> *Ain't she sweet?*

She would return and take her bows, doing a curtsy with her apron. Then I might sing to her:

> *You ought to be in pictures.*
> *You're beautiful to see.*
> *You ought to be in pictures.*
> *Oh, what a hit you would be!*

Half a dozen times a day she would have to break off work to answer a knock at the door. In those days when few women drove a car, peddlers came to them. Milk, butter, eggs, ice were still delivered in horse-drawn wagons, only beginning to give way to delivery trucks. In addition to these regular deliverymen came peddlers selling rugs, lace doilies, hangings depicting Indian princesses and Bedouin sheiks printed in primary colors on purple or black velveteen, furniture polish, cosmetics, kitchen utensils, home remedies, Bibles. The coming of one kind of door-to-door salesman, which usually gladdened my mother, saddened her that summer. This was the itinerant photographers who worked the street with a saddled Shetland pony or a brightly painted cart drawn by a billygoat or a big St. Bernard dog. My mother had never been able to resist having my picture taken by one of these. She would scour the neighborhood to find me at my play whenever she saw one wending our way.

Sometimes when she did not know I was watching her at her work through the doorway, my mother's song would trail off and worry would sadden her face. I, too, was subject to moods from out of nowhere, and, rooted to my spot, was shaken sometimes as though by a sudden gust of cold wind. I could not choose which of my playthings to play with—instantly I wanted none of them. I was tired of them all, I hated them, and felt like sweeping them off the bed to break on the floor. My bones ached from immobility. I shook with impatience at my helplessness.

Then I would lose touch with myself. Try to remember myself in clothes. Out of doors. At school. In the woods. On the square. Playing on the plaza around the monument. Once this started it was not to be reversed— as irresistible as the pull of gravity. The walls of this room where I was trapped closed in. The bed engulfed me. I was in over my head. I went down once, twice. My mother, never far away, would come running at my cry and hug me to her until I had sobbed myself out.

But I was really very lucky, as another category of my mother's songs, one that she had brought with her to town from the country, taught me. Very different these were from the catchy, light-hearted popular tunes she got from the radio and which everybody sang. These were like old songs of home that an exile might sing in times of homesickness, not to cheer herself, but to mourn, pitched to a near-sob and frequently breaking into one, with a nasal, almost adenoidal whine to them, and almost in another tongue, requiring a lapse from my mother's acquired, refined, town speech into a dialect at once more literary and more down to earth. These plaintive ballads both frightened me and made me feel that I was lucky, that I was secure from the fickleness and cruelty and loneliness of the world they depicted. In those songs, only disappointment could be counted on. Fortune smiled fleetingly only to frown lastingly on you. Lovers all proved false. Friends deserted you when fortune did. The main business of big cities was luring and corrupting country boys. The only person who ever truly loved you was your mother—more than you deserved, more than you appreciated until it was too late. I marvelled, even as a child, that songwriters, every mother's son of them, seemed to have been the product of virgin birth, supposedly so uncommon: there was seldom a musical mention of dear old dad, unless it was to want a girl just like the girl who married him.

I was lucky. I had my mother and I had Clarksville. I would stick with both, I would never go down to the railroad and catch myself a midnight train, beat my way to Georgia, land in a gambling town, get myself in trouble, shoot a country sheriff down, be taken to Atlanta and tied to a ball and chain.

Life was luck. Examples of the unlucky were all around me: black faces, the friendless deaf-mute, Dummy, in the cobbler's shop and his young assistant who had lost a leg in a shooting accident; one-armed Mr. Jap Barry; my own downtrodden, dispirited grandfather —to remind me how lucky I was. How lucky that my father possessed the skill which had saved me from a life like his own as a child! I was bedridden for a time now, but think of Cleo Kelty strapped to her bedboard for life. I had lived through a cyclone that killed a dozen people, had picked up the house I was in and moved it a hundred yards. For close calls: how many other nine-year-olds could show you their signed death certificates? Why, there was hardly another boy in the world as lucky as I was. It made me feel sorry for all the others. In later years a close friend of mine told me how blessed he felt that he was a Jew. He pitied me and all the other poor misbegotten gentiles in the restaurant where he made me this declaration. His Jewishness sustained him every minute of his life. As a boy I felt that way about my luckiness: I was then one of the chosen race.

On top of her usual housework, which to my mother meant sweeping, dusting and mopping everything every day, preparing three hot meals including biscuits for each of them and two fresh-baked pies daily, and tending to me, trying to keep me entertained, forecasting and heading off my black moods and cooking me special treats (I learned to like to eat that summer in bed— something I had always been too much on the go for before), my mother was busy all that time canning.

She canned every summer—the quilting frame that hung suspended by pulleys over the dining table was never lowered then; but never before had she canned on such a scale as that year. Never before had the times so demanded it. The depression, the drought, the dust storms had brought us low. More and more of my father's customers were unable to pay what they owed him, and we had the new burden of my doctor's bills (and the prospect of future operations and therapy, though I knew nothing about this). My mother invested in dozens more Mason jars, bought sugar by the hundred-pound bag, ran up the biggest gas bill ever, but figured that she would still save us a great deal of money.

She canned whatever the day brought, whatever the farmer brought whose cry, accompanied by the clop of his horses' hooves, we heard that morning from down at the foot of the street. That summer the farmer and the farmer's boy would sometimes have to make three trips from the wagon to our kitchen to tote in all that my mother had bought.

She would be aglow with triumph over the bargain she had struck and the fine quality of the produce. Being a mother, living in town, keeping house, shopping were still new and exciting to her. "Sweetcorn today," she would announce, bringing a bushel basketful of it into my room. "Just look!" peeling back a tassel. "Don't that make your mouth water! The tomatoes looked real good, too, but they'll keep. They'll be in season for a good while yet, and if I wait I think the price will go still lower. I'll take my chance on that. But right now is the time for sweetcorn!" As many as four or five bushels she would have, all to be shucked, boiled, cut from the cob. Whatever it was to be peeled or shelled, she did it, to keep me company, in my room. So I cannot claim not to have known how much work her canning that summer cost her. Alone in the house with her all day, I was the sole witness to it.

The little bungalow steamed. From morning till night the range had all burners going, boiling the vegetables and sterilizing the jars and caps, baking, cooking the meals. It was hot outside, hot in my room—the kitchen was an oven. When my mother broke off her work to answer a call from me, or to check to see why she had

had no such call for some time, her face was flushed red, her red hair straggling in her hurry to get done all that she had set herself to do. As each came ripe, she put up peas, beans, greens, tomatoes, beets, pickles, relishes, cherries, plums, pears, peaches, apples. We would have nothing to buy all winter, and our food would be home-cooked. She canned so much there was no place to store it. So my father bought lumber and spent three Sundays lining the garage with shelves.

My luck held. In early fall the bandages were removed. Not knowing that I could never do it again, I bent my knee, and have been doing so ever since. The doctor was better than he knew. I was unsteady on my feet from long lying down, but I soon remedied that. The ugly scar impressed my classmates, and earned me a great many nickels at my reappearance on the square.

Another crop came in now, and it too was stored in the garage: nuts. These came from customers of my father, farmers who paid him a little on what they owed him with an occasional country-cured ham, a dozen eggs, a bit of fresh pork at hog-killing time, a gallon of sorghum syrup, or, knowing his boy's insatiable appetite for them, a towsackful of pecans, black walnuts.

There in the garage one day that fall, surrounded by my mother's glistening jars of fruit and vegetables, I was cracking walnuts with a hammer on the concrete floor when I squashed my thumb. Really squashed it—lost the nail, which grows unevenly to this day. But if I had lost the thumb itself it would hardly justify or explain my doing what I did. Were I to be tried for it, temporary insanity would have to be my plea. When I came out of it, I found myself spattered all over standing on a floor awash with peaches, beans, tomatoes, broken glass.

I had smashed with my hammer every jar within reach of my mother's canning, on which I had watched her work all summer, on which she had spent what was for us a large sum of money, and which was to have fed us all winter. I was appalled—more afraid of myself than I was of what she might do to me. Unused to punishment though I was, this time I fully expected my mother to flay me alive, disown me, have me sent to the reformatory, and I believed I deserved it all.

I was not punished. When I saw that I was not to be, then I longed to be. Not to be was truly to be disowned, put beyond the pale. I had committed such an enormity that no punishment was adequate to it. My mother's sorrow at her loss, and her fright and dismay at the devil that had gotten into her only child, whom she had nursed so devotedly, was a punishment that I feel to this day.

THIS TIME it was a sprained ankle. That was all it was. No bones were broken, no blood shed. It was embarrassing to a boy of my age for his mother to baby him in front of the two playmates who had helped him hobble home. Even a bad sprain—and this one was looking worse by the minute—was still only a sprain, after all. Nothing like as bad as the time I cut my knee.

I was always getting hurt. Being little and forced to run to keep up with the boys, all of whom, overnight, were shooting up Texan-tall, and, even when off playing by myself, adventurous and careless, I always had a bandage on me somewhere or other, a stubbed toe, a scab on an elbow or a knee, or both, or all four. I was as scarred as an old soldier. A sprain was about the only injury I had not had before.

But often as it happened, my mother could never harden herself to any hurt sustained by her one and only baby boy. None was even taken lightly. To belittle a hurt, especially those that *were* little, was to get my mother started. It was worse than it looked, you could be sure of that; in any case, unless it was taken seriously and treated accordingly . . . Well, remember President Coolidge's poor boy. Dead of blood poisoning which all began with a blister on his heel. Think of that the next time you got one from breaking in a new pair of shoes! Remember Mrs. Thatcher, our one-time neighbor. In opening a can, an ordinary tin can, a can of Del Monte's creamed corn, she pounded the handle of the can-opener a little hard, bruised her palm, paid no attention to it—and where was Mrs. Thatcher now? (She was dead, aged thirty-seven, having been amputated joint by joint, beginning with that bruised hand.) This time I and my two human crutches had barely rounded the corner onto my street when my mother came flying the two blocks to meet us. It was as though she had been sitting at the window keeping watch, in dread of this very thing. You would have thought I had been brought home lamed for life. My mother behaved as though this was worse than the time I cut my knee.

When my shoe had been eased off and my sock cut away, the sight of my foot was enough to sober me; it almost undid my mother. While I soaked it in ice-water, she got on the phone. She called the doctor. She called my father. She called her oldest sister, in Dallas. Long-distance calls, in our house, were reserved for important

—meaning disastrous—occasions. Having done all this, my mother seemed not to know what to do with herself. She took another look at the foot, gave a cry, and called the doctor and my father again.

"It's only a sprain, Mother," I kept telling her—telling myself. Because she was frightening me now. It was my first one but I had seen others, and those boys' mothers had said to them, "Well, it could have been worse. It's only a sprain." Mine, of course, always made a great fuss whenever I got hurt; the way she was taking on now, though, seemed excessive even for her. The chill mounted steadily from my foot by way of my marrow.

It was time to freshen the ice-water. With a shake of her head and an irrepressible gasp, my mother took away the pan. In replacing it, she got down on her knees. Once there, she seemed unable to get up again, to tear herself away from the sight of my foot, which now had lost all likeness to a foot and resembled, as nearly as anything, an eggplant: that color, that size, shape, and, despite the soaking, with skin, stretched by the blood from the broken vessels, that glossy taut. My mother bent over still further and began to shake with silent, unutterable sobs. The chill reached my heart.

When she was able to talk, my mother, still without rising or even looking up, poured out to me a confession of guilt which had burdened her from the moment I was born. A guilt which explained why she had pampered and spoiled me as she had—and which made all that indulgence even more undeserved. All the more touching because it was uncalled for, her suffering was the bitter fruit of ignorance, of a young country girl's trust in the word of older country women as ignorant as she was.

I listened in amazement as my mother revealed to me that I had been born crippled. I, who since I learned to walk, had never walked when I could run—crippled? Badly so—hopelessly so, was the general judgment. That same right foot of mine, now turned downward at an unnatural angle, had been turned up when I was born and lay flat against my shin. Her first child, a hard delivery, and she just nineteen. She had not stopped crying over me for the first six months of my life.

No wonder she never liked to talk about the house I was born in. Surely she was not sorry that it had been torn down.

It was her fault, all her fault, and I would grow up to hate her and to curse her to her face. She had been told to sleep always on her back, warned that if she slept often on her side something like this could happen. She tried to obey but it was as if their telling her that had put a devil in her. She would stretch herself out on her back and before she knew it she had rolled over. She would stiffen herself and lie as rigid as a corpse, resist every temptation to turn over, finally, in exhaustion, drop off to sleep, then wake, in terror, lying on her side —on me. She almost knew to expect it when I was born as I was.

For people of our class, misfortunes like me were accepted as the judgment of God and left to grow up as best they could. Lucky for me that my mother was not typical of her class! The driving force of her life had been to lift herself out of it and to shed every tell-tale trace of her origins. Any reminder of them from anybody rubbed her fur the wrong way and brought her claws out. She was in lifelong rebellion against that passive acceptance of inferiority and second-class rights. To this streak of independence and pride in my mother I owe the fact that I have not gone through life lame. She dared to demand for her child the right to the best medical treatment available. Her search for it took her all the way to Dallas, and there she found a doctor who believed he could alleviate, possibly even correct, my deformity. If she had not been ashamed to tell him, he might, with a word, have cured her of the notion that she had caused it by sleeping on her side. She may well have believed that he knew she had done that without her confessing it. This doctor fitted me with a series of braces graduated to bring the still soft and pliable bones more nearly into proper place. By the time I was three, the bones had firmed and set in their places, and the last brace was removed. Not only had I never walked with the least limp, I had never known until now that anything had ever been wrong with me.

But my poor mother had lived always in fear that the ankle would fail me. When I had gotten safely up to nine on it, and she was just about to release the breath she had held all that long, I cut the knee of that same leg and once again she was told that I would be lame for life.

I tried to visualize that crippled baby I had been. The image that came to me was from my baby pictures. In all of them, I realized now, my right leg, the one with the brace, is tucked out of sight beneath my skirt. I pitied my poor young mother for having a baby whom she had partly to hide, and always with the sense of guilt toward him, toward his father, and toward the world, that a self-indulgence of hers was responsible for his defect.

I understood now why my mother had never given

me the baby brother or sister I had so often begged her for. And I realized how painful to her my begging must have been, revivifying the memory of her troubles with me.

A good thing she hadn't, for there would now be still another mouth for her to feed, I thought as I sat staring at that house where I learned all this and which had re-arisen on its charred foundation out of the heat waves that throbbed above the pavement of the street, like a mirage.

MY MOTHER took very seriously her responsibility to feed her family and she worked hard on every meal she served. Food was the one expense she would not scrimp on. She shopped shrewdly, buying the best and making sure that it *was* the best. The butcher took pains with her order, though, with all the game we ate, she was far from being his best customer, and he heard from her when a cut of meat fell short of her expectations. She was an excellent cook, yet she never sat down to a meal without a certain anxious little smile, eager that her efforts be appreciated, apprehensive at the last minute that despite all her care something might have gone wrong. After my father and I had tasted everything and complimented her on it, only then could she enjoy her meal. Assured of our praise, she could afford, before it was done, to find some fault with every dish. If one escaped her criticism, she might say, as we were complimenting her one last time before going to bed, "I thought the limas were just a little bit tough."

As she was so conscientious and hard-working, it was a great disappointment to my mother whenever, as happened all too often, a meal was delayed by my father's having to answer a call to repair a car broken down on the road. Sometimes he was kept so late that she and I ate without him. She ate little then. Later, serving him his warmed-over meal, she was so apologetic about it, lamenting how good this and that *had* been, that it was a wonder he could get down a bite of it, that she did not spoil his appetite altogether.

The meal of the week that my mother sat down to always with the keenest anticipation and, consequently, the keenest anxiety was Sunday dinner—meaning the midday meal. Into it went the most money, the most planning, the most time and work, and from it came the most enjoyment. It was the meal on which, no matter whose car broke down, my father was expected to tell him firmly that he must wait.

Rare as the occurrence was, however, I was not much surprised one Sunday when my father did not come home to dinner in the house on Third Street. I, meteorologist of the domestic weather, had checked my instruments first thing that morning and had found all gauges indicating *storm.*

The living room sofa bore the impress of my father's having spent the night there. As when a cloud cover hangs low overhead, sounds—such sounds as were made—were magnified that morning. Breakfast was eaten in such heavy silence that the occasional remark seemed thunderous. As soon as it was over, my father quit the house with a slamming of doors, a blast of the car engine and a sound from his tires on the street like the rip of a buzz saw.

Grim-lipped and silent, as though it was poison she was preparing, my mother cooked the dinner, fixing a meal that would be a reproach in itself, a meal fit for a king in order to show him just how far removed from that estate he was. Actually, for a reason presently to be explained, I do not remember what she made, except for the first course—only that into it went all her considerable art, and that it was seasoned with all her considerable spite.

When everything was in the oven that should be in it and everything out of it that should be out, my mother untied her apron, tidied herself and changed into her Sunday clothes. For the occasion, she wore a necklace of pearls, painted glass pearls. I, too, changed into my Sunday best.

Two o'clock, the appointed, the accustomed, the consecrated hour neared, came, and went without my father's appearing. The silent street carried no sound of a car. My mother began to hum—infallible signal of an approaching squall.

The oven and the burners of the stove were turned low and lids were put on pots to keep their contents warm—and a cover put on my mother's anger to keep it simmering. Restrained from work or play by our clothes, and by our mood, she and I sat stiffly attending. It was always when she was most hurt that my mother was the most composed. Too composed. I knew well that will of hers not to let her hurt be seen by whoever had caused it, and the pain and resentment it masked. I knew to dread the wounded, reproachful and unforgiving silence she emanated at such times. The minutes that were passing did so without affecting her expression or her prideful bearing, but I knew that each of them was another double-distilled drop in her cup of bitterness.

My joints were stiff from sitting, my appetite entirely gone and the very thought of food hateful to me when my mother declared that we would wait no longer but would eat our dinner now, "ruined though it was." The first course of our long-delayed meal that day was soup. She ladled out the soup, her homemade tomato soup—"the beautiful red soup in the gray plate": years later, those words, in Katherine Mansfield's "Bliss," the story of a day in a life that will turn from bliss to bale before it is over, would leap off the page at me, and I would surely be her one reader for whom the line of verse which she intends as a parody on modern poetry, "Why must it always be tomato soup?" missed her satiric aim. There would be real poignancy in that plaint for me, for after that day in my life it would seem that for me it always was tomato soup, a dish which still rouses in me painful memories.

A car going far too fast made the turn onto our street, down at the foot. Catching my breath, I arrested the spoon I was lifting to my lips. I lowered it a notch as I listened to the speed with which the car was coming toward us. Into our driveway it plunged and braked to a sudden stop. I returned my spoon, full, to my plate.

"Eat," said my mother, doing so herself.

The front door slammed. Something, knocked against, fell and clattered, and was cursed for being in the way. I bowed my head over my plate. I wished I was somewhere else, away from this tension and strife, this unhappiness.

"Eating without me?" my father said.

My mother, glancing up at the clock on the wall, said nothing. In his present condition, he was a stranger to her, so said her manner, and she urged me with a look to go on with my dinner and ignore the man. She always began a fight by acting above the fray, as though contrasting her refinement to his crudity. This never lasted long; she could, and soon did, turn just as low-down rough as he.

"Well, no hurry about it," said my father. "A man needs to work up an appetite for a meal in this atmosphere."

"If you know another one more to your liking—"

How could they not see how unhappy they were making me and stop it, both of them? Did they not love me enough to love each other any more?

"Any other! Any at all! You're the one who makes me say it. It's you who drives me away."

"And me that drives you to come reeling home, a shame and a disgrace to your own child? Is that me, too?"

Oh, how I wished she would leave me out of it!

It was then that, with a growl in his throat, he lunged for her. She rose from the table, knocking over her chair. I rose, too. He swung, striking her a blow on the head that sent her staggering to the wall. I screamed. Blind now with rage, and goaded on by very shame of what he was doing, he went after her, and I, blind with pain, went after him. As he hit her, I hit him with all my puny strength. He grabbed at her and caught her string of pearls. The string broke, the beads peppering the walls, the ceiling, landing on the quilt in its frame. That stopped him, and the three of us stood aghast, panting for breath. My father muttered a curse and quit the room. I heard the springs of the sofa sag as he threw himself heavily upon it.

My mother smoothed herself and patted her hair back

into place. She cleared her throat. She righted her chair, sat down at the table and motioned me to take my place.

"Eat your dinner," she said.

The spoon shook as I conveyed it to my lips. My teeth were clenched to keep them from chattering. I was seized and shaken by an uncontrollable trembling. The least thing further and I would break down. My feeling was that I had failed in the thing I had been born for, to keep my parents united and happy with each other.

Something was in the spoonful of soup I forced into my mouth. I removed it. It was one of my mother's pearls. In just a moment I was going to be sick. I laid it on the cloth beside my plate. I managed to say, "May I be excused, please?" Without waiting for an answer, I rose from the table and left the house. After being sick behind the garage, I ran until I could run no farther.

WHEN THE HOUSE ON THIRD STREET BURNED, it burned to the ground. Nothing we owned was saved from the conflagration. We ourselves were spared by being away from home that weekend on a visit to friends in Texarkana. We returned to a smouldering bed of cinders.

Even my hobbyhorse burned, and it was not in the house, but hanging from a limb of the tree across the driveway from it. This was the loss I felt most keenly, for my hobbyhorse was no ordinary one. Far from it. Mine was unique, irreplaceable. Its size, beauty and rarity, and the strangeness of my finding it, had made my hobbyhorse almost magical to me.

It was, when I first saw it, one of a whole herd of hobbyhorses, in a field, in a circle, as though, with flying hooves, racing one another around a track. It was early one Sunday morning, on a highway not far outside Clarksville, when we came upon this astonishing sight. It was a merry-go-round, a very old merry-go-round— so old it looked as though it had stood in that field, exposed to the weather, peeling and rusting, for years. Yet, as we knew, it had not been there just the day before.

There were a dozen large wooden horses, no two exactly alike, hand-carved, with outstretched fore- and hindlegs, streaming manes, full flowing tails. Most of the paint was gone from them. Some were cracked where the joints in the wood had split and warped apart. Some were missing a leg or a portion of the tail. Some were blind, others half blind—one or both of their glass eyes gone. But those that had them both seemed to plead with them to be saved, ridden again. Looking out from their faded, flaking, wood-grained bodies, their artificial eyes seemed deep with life.

How had they gotten there? Clarksville had had no fair, no carnival, no passing entertainment of any sort recently. What was this strange, exotic thing, a discarded merry-go-round, doing in this empty pasture? It might have fallen from the skies. My father speculated that some poor, fly-by-night little road-show had come to the end of the line at this spot. Maybe some wheezy old truck had finally balked at its load. Maybe some dispute had split up the troupe. Or maybe in a moment of clearheadedness the owner had had enough of a vagabond and hand-to-mouth existence with attractions as outmoded as this battered, paintless, laughable, pitiful old merry-go-round.

Whatever the explanation, it was plain to see that the thing had been abandoned there, that it was any-

body's for the taking, and we were the first on the scene.
I wanted them all; as instructed, I chose one—the best
one. My father freed it from its iron post with a hack-
saw. He took it to his shop, and before the day was over
he had transformed it into a fiery black mustang with
a red saddle, bridle reins, stirrups which he forged from
old car parts and hung on straps.

When he stood back and admired what he had done
with the one, my father changed his mind and decided
that I had been right in wanting them all. Or rather,
what he decided was that he could repair, repaint and
sell the other ones.

It was early evening when we arrived, by truck, and
carrying an acetylene cutting torch, back at the spot.
The merry-go-round had vanished, leaving no trace. Had
its owner reconsidered and come back to reclaim it—
minus its finest specimen? We never learned. I never
knew another child except myself who had gotten one
of them. Being unique, my hobbyhorse became almost
a children's institution in Clarksville, and its loss was
mourned not just by me, but publicly.

THE BURNING of one thing in that fire, it seemed to
me now, as I sat staring across the street at where our
house had stood, at the charred foundation which was
all that was left of it, was prophetic. This was a piece
of paper. A death certificate. My own, stating that, aged
seven, I had died of "accidental suffocation . . ."

THE THREE sizeable lakes near Clarksville were all
privately owned by associations; their composition re-
flected the upper, middle and lower classes of the town.

At the top was exclusive North Lake. Membership there was not even by invitation but by inheritance; it came with the cottages, bigger and better built than many year-round houses in town, each on its several acres, that graced its shores. South Lake was the middle rung; to it belonged young professional and businessmen on the rise who were screened and kept waiting for a while before being invited to join, and for whom it was important not only as a place to get out of town and cool off with a swim on sweltering summer evenings and drink bootleg liquor, but for establishing status and combining business with pleasure. No invitation was needed to belong to Crystal Lake—farther from town, working class, rough, with a big old unpainted club-house with a big dance hall, bedrooms without plumbing furnished with army cots, and a tin-roofed open-sided shed with trestle tables to eat at. Membership in Crystal Lake was anybody's for a small annual subscription. We had one the summer I turned seven.

I loved Crystal Lake once I was there, but getting there was a trial for me, as getting anywhere was; for in this I was not my father's son: I had only to look at a car to get carsick—we called what I got "the colic." On long trips I was dosed—doped—with paregoric; short ones, though they seemed long to me, I just had to suffer through. At the time, I lacked the experience to make the comparison, but the trip to Crystal Lake, in a model A Ford sprung as stiff and unyielding as a cottonwagon, over unpaved roads rutted by the spring rains, was like a stormy crossing of the sea. I spent it, between stops for me to get out and throw up, lying on the back seat. It was said—had been all my life—that this was a phase I would grow out of.

With us, most years, it was warm enough for swimming by late March. That was hardly soon enough for my father, who, around water, was still a boy at heart, and who pointed to his half-webbed second and third toes as proof that he was part water-bird. We would leave town on Saturday afternoons that spring and summer as soon as he got off work and scrubbed the grease off him, and would arrive at the lake at sundown. All the members, all wage earners or self-employed tradesmen, arrived together. While the wives unpacked the cars and started fires to warm the supper, the children ran wild, me among them, sick as I had been just minutes earlier. The men repaired together to the woods, from which they returned smelling as though they had come fresh from the barber shop.

My father was unofficial fisherman of Crystal Lake Club. For as a fisherman my father was no more of a sportsman than as a hunter. He was far too restless a man for fishing in the way it was done for sport in our parts. In that country of slow—if not still—murky, warm waters, and the sluggish varieties of fish they bred, fishing was a sedentary pastime, done mainly by old women in straw hats with cane poles sitting on railroad trestles offering worms or live minnows to perch, catfish and bream. At Crystal Lake the fishing was for meat.

We, my father and I, strung a trotline baited with minnows from one shore of the lake to the other. When the trotline was set, we turned and rowed back in the deepening dusk toward the flames of the cooking grill and the lamplights beginning to glow from the windows of the clubhouse. The warm water steamed in the chill of the evening and the bullfrogs were in full chorus, sounding like the bass strings of bass fiddles being bowed, tuning themselves to one another.

"Go gigging them tonight, maybe," my father would say.

Although I had never seen that done, I knew about it. I had seen the carbide headlamps, like miners', that the men wore and the three-tined, barbed spears on long cane poles with which they gigged the frogs dazzled by the lights. To me it meant froglegs for breakfast. Everybody always had to watch as they cooked, kicking in the skillet to the last.

Supper was a little bit of lots of different things: what each woman had brought from home and all shared. Afterwards, it was never long before somebody cranked up the Victrola and put a record on. I was allowed to stay up and watch for a little while before being put to bed. I loved seeing my father and mother dance together, their grace as they twirled to the music and glided all around the big hall. I loved the pair they made. Powdered wax strewn on the floor rose around their ankles and sparkled like dew from the grass when it is walked through early in the morning. It was to the sound of Gene Austin and another singer who, though new, was already my mother's favorite, Bing Crosby, and the shuffle of feet on the dance floor, that the young ones like me went to sleep in their cots.

I would be wakened by a touch, maybe a shake, to see my father bending over me with his finger to his lips. Day would be just breaking. We dressed and tip-toed from the room carrying our shoes. To trick my mother while she slept and slip off without her knowing was fun when it was done with my father. It made us two boys. I would be sleepy but glad to be up. I loved my father's wanting me with him, just me. Times like this when he and I were alone together were the ones I treasured most. Out together with him while everybody else slept, I felt that the world belonged to us.

Steam rising from the lake as it warmed in the early sun made it look as though it had just been ladled there to cool. At our appearance, ducks beat the water and lifted into the mist. "Mallards," my father would say, or "Teal"—training me for the time when I would shoot them with him. At the dock my father would lift me and swing me over and set me in the boat, then launch us. He fitted the oars in the locks, dipped them, and we sliced through the water—a sensation that always brought me a delight so intense I had to laugh.

We rowed to shore. There an end of the trotline rose out of the water to the stake it was tied to. My father untied it and lifted it as high as he could. He lifted a hundred feet of it out of the water. Perfect as a necklace it was, a fish to a hook, glinting in the sunlight like polished silver.

We ran the line, unhooking the fish and tossing them to flop together in the tub. Lunch that day was a fishfry for all on which everybody feasted.

Watching my parents swim out to the float in the middle of the lake both thrilled and frightened me. I had no fear that either of them might not make it to the float; both were good swimmers, my father an expert one. I had little if any conception of what the alternative to their making it would be. The fear for me came simply from being left on shore and separated from them by a medium which I could not negotiate at all. They looked so small, waving back to me from away out there. And that made me feel even smaller than I was.

My favorite cousin, Ramsay Floyd, only son of my favorite aunt, my mother's sister Mildred, was on a visit to us and was brought with us to Crystal Lake that weekend. Before it was over, Ramsay was to become more my favorite than ever—the most important person to me since my parents had made me. That was the weekend when I nearly lost my life; indeed, according to the available medical opinion, I had lost it. But when everybody else had given up on it, Ramsay was to give it back to me.

Ramsay was not his name, which was Wallace, but a nickname, and now that he was twelve going on thirteen everybody in the family but me had stopped calling him by it. But though he might have outgrown the name, he had not outgrown the trait which had earned it for him. Something about the truth was a challenge to that boy; he could no more leave it alone than a dog could pass by a bush—he had to put his mark on it. He was not vicious, did not mean to mislead—by now he never expected to be believed, in any case; just that a fact, with its hard edges, grated him, and so around it he spun a pearl. It was our English grandfather who had nicknamed him. After listening to one of Wallace's whoppers, that double-dyed Tory said, "Bigger liar than Ramsay MacDonald, that boy." To which Ramsay, whose grin was so fixed that he must have slept with it, grinned a little wider.

While my parents swam out to the float, I was left, in Ramsay's charge, to play in the kiddy-pen. The kiddy-pen was a floating big box in the water, made of wood, with an inclined bottom, slanting from a depth shallow enough for toddlers to wade to a depth of about five feet. It happened that day that I had it all to myself. Ramsay swam outside it, returning often to look over the sides and make sure that I was all right.

I was all right so long as I just floated in my lifesaver innertube or jumped feet first off the sides. How even at the age of seven I could have been so stupid as not to realize that should I dive head-first I would dive out of my innertube, I do not know, but that is what I did, and when I came up I could not find it again.

I surfaced screaming for help but I made no sound, for my voice was drowned already. I groped in the air for something to grasp hold of. I sank, and a murky greenness flooded my brain. The pressure on my chest was crushing. I rose again, sank again. The sensation of greenness behind and before my eyes made it seem as though my entire body was absorbing water in between all its cells, like a sponge. I grew heavier, and this heaviness drew me down, down. The instinct to hold my breath failed me and my desperate lungs filled with the alien element. I surfaced one last time, sank for the last time. In swift succession as I sank I knew I was dying, knew I was dead, knew nothing.

Having died and been brought back to life, I found it not so very strange that the world should be upside down, that mine should be the newborn baby's view of things. I was being held in the air by my heels and shaken like a balky bottle of ketchup to get it to pour, and from me—from my lungs, my stomach, my ears, my eyes—the scalding water streamed. The greenness inside my head ebbed away (but leaving an ineradicable memory of itself, like the stain on building walls left by the high-water mark in a flood, a memory that, more nights than not, returns at the moment I am about to drift into what the French call the little death of sleep, and wakens me gasping with terror; for, as time, since I learned to tell time, is reddish for me, so out-of-time, unconsciousness, death—which I learned of at about the same time—is that watery, dim-lit green). It was Ramsay who had pulled me out. It was Ramsay, sobbing frantically, wild with the thought that his momentary negligence of me was responsible, and despairing at the failure of his Boy Scout training efforts to resuscitate me, who was holding me in the air by the heels and shaking me up and down.

I had died and been brought back from the dead, revived by a child, by the time my parents swam ashore from the float. Had Ramsay listened to the grownups who gathered over me, and particularly to Dr. Carlton, I would not be writing this. The debt has not been interest-free, but I have been living since the age of seven on borrowed time, and it was Ramsay who got me the loan. The seldom-sober Dr. Carlton—he who had very nearly killed me himself just the year before with an overdose of ether while drunkenly extracting my tonsils, and who was there that weekend as the guest of one of the members—had listened to my heart, felt my pulse, and, being the County Coroner, had taken from his bag his handy pad of death certificates and filled out mine. I kept it—I treasured it—until, along with everything else of mine except the clothes I had on, it burned. It was my talisman—official proof that I led a charmed life.

Its burning was added proof that I did. I had not been in the house to burn with it.

Now I half wished I had been.

The body was delivered from the undertaker's at the end of the day, at the hour when men who lived on Third Street, our former neighbors, were getting home from work. Mr. Hess, Mr. Gray, Mr. Storey—James's father—Mr. Sales: I had seen them all go by in the past few minutes. From my post at the window I now saw the hearse appear at the end of the street and watched it bear down on us like a boat coming into its berth. It ran as silently as though its engine had been cut. It had been serviced regularly by my father, and he could never tolerate the least squeak or rattle in a car in his care. One in his own car affected him like a leaky faucet in the night, and one of my most familiar images was of him lying on the hood or the fender or the running board while my mother drove, trying to locate the noise that offended him and which I could not even hear. He had had the hearse in his shop for a tune-up only the other day. Indeed, he was its first passenger since his work on it; this I had overheard, for it was one of those ironies that people remarked on in times like this. To escape from such observations was one more of my reasons for secluding myself.

The coffin was slid out the back door of the hearse onto its carriage and wheeled up the walk. It was lifted up the porch steps. I heard the rotation of the wheels on the planks of the porch, the lifting over the doorsill, and the maneuvering into the living room.

As I was expecting, my mother entered the room. Her

eyes were red and swollen, her features puffed, her chin puckered and her lips continually twitching.

"You can come see him now," she said.

"No," I said.

"He's not . . . I mean, they've fixed him up. Real nice. He's . . ."

I shook my head.

Tears filled my mother's eyes. She was exhausted. On top of everything else, now this. Instead of being a comfort and a support to her, I was adding to her troubles.

"I don't want to see," I said. "I'm not going." Between my two declarations the pause was short, but the difference in tone was striking—enough so as to make us both stare. The first had been spoken by a boy, the second by a man, as though in between them my voice had broken.

A look different from any other we had ever exchanged passed then between my mother and me, one that put a new distance between us. She did not try to look me down, to glare me into obedience as she had always done before when I was acting stubborn and contrary. Suddenly we had gone past that. We had reached a parting of ways. Just when we needed each other most, I had detached my hand from hers and set off on my own path. But I was not being willful, I was being myself, the new self that I had yet to learn. My mother knew better than I did that life was a succession of severances. I had come into the world when my time in her womb was up; now that I was being delivered from this little womb of a world into the larger one, another cord must be cut.

My mother accepted silently my declaration of independence. She was in too weak a state to protest. She pitied me too much to command me against my will. She feared to test her power of command over me. My independence underlined fears she had already begun to feel. Nothing yet had brought home to her more forcibly the fact that she was now a widow. She no longer had my father to appeal to for authority when I disobeyed or disputed her. Already she was being treated with the world's diminished regard for a woman without a man—and now by her own, her only child. There was no doubt that my mother had lost some of my respect by losing her husband, just as I sensed that I myself had lost the respect of others by losing my father.

IN OUR FAMILY OF LITTLE PEOPLE a saying frequently on our lips was, Diamonds come in small packages—also that dynamite did. It was impossible now to believe that so much zest for living as was crammed into that small, explosive package, my father, could have been snuffed out. He had been as positive a presence as a rambunctious boy, snatching at life with both hands. He was one of those to leave his name on every place he went: *Clarence Humphrey was here.* Such intensity as that with which he went at everything, the fieriness of his feelings, his avidity for sensation and experience: how could all that have been extinguished? He was still too young, too nimble, still too quick on his feet, for even this strong challenger—tough, wary, a scrapper, always with his mitts up; one would have thought that death could not so soon have found an opening in his defenses.

Death at the wheel of a car? Clarence Humphrey? In a place where people prided themselves on being good drivers, by which they meant fast drivers, Clarence Humphrey handled a car with the ease and command with which other men handled their knife and fork. Death on a road he knew like he knew the part in his hair?

"Ah, well," I could hear them saying down at the garage, where his wrecked car, like all the others before it, had been towed and was now on view, "it can happen to the best." *Accordioned*, the car was said to be. Where, when, by whom I had heard that said sometime during these past days, I did not know.

While I sat in my room alone, relatives and friends of the family came for a last look at my father's body. People came in large numbers. My mother was amazed at the outpouring, and she got some satisfaction out of this, the last occasion for pride in her man that he would ever provide her. Yet of many who came to call she was bound to say after he was gone, "Be more comfort to me if he would pay me the money he's owed Clarence for years."

By evening the queue of cars parked in the street stretched out of sight around the furthermost corners. The people, all dressed in black or in their most somber clothes, gathered on the lawn. Their very number was meant to be and ought to have been a comfort to me— it was the opposite. I knew I was being unreasonable, and yet the greater the number of people who came to condole with us on our misfortune, the greater our misfortune seemed to me. The more children with their fathers assembled outside the house, the more capricious and cruel seemed my being singled out to lose mine. They spoke, when they spoke at all, in low voices. They heaved frequent sighs—of sadness, of shortness of breath in the stifling heat. They shook their heads often. That would be over my mother and me.

Among those who came to the house—he to the back yard, where he stood alone, bowed in his grief—was Wylie, and not even him would I see. Him least of all. With him I would surely have lost my self-command and begun to cry. Once started, I would not be able to stop. That suffering must be borne alone was what I was learning, and that in solitude lay the sole hope of surviving it.

For the rest of the world, my father was dead; for me, he refused to die.

I have said that he loved to swim and that he was a strong and expert swimmer. One of my most vivid and most intimate images of the two of us together was of him floating on his back, as he could do effortlessly and by the hour, with me straddling his stomach; I had done it times out of number. This image haunted me now, only now he was sinking, clinging to me—me, the non-swimmer—to keep us afloat, get us to shore.

He could glide through the woods in those old tennis shoes he hunted in as silent as a shadow. How many times had I, so much smaller and lighter than he, followed in his footsteps, treading on every twig he had avoided! He could stand immobile by the hour—I, meanwhile, fidgeting, sighing, sneezing—to outlast the wariness of his hidden quarry. Now that he lay silenced and stilled forever, that silence and stillness of his haunted my memory—or rather, some portion of me far too real, too present, too persistent to be called memory.

With few men, surely, was ever such a repertory of smells associated: those of his trade and those of his sports: gunpowder and gunpowder solvent, the different scents of the various species of game, citronella, suntan lotion to protect his fair skin, muriatic acid, the special soap with which he scrubbed the grease off his hands, gasoline, acetylene, the banana-odor of the lacquer he sprayed on car bodies—to instance only a few; now, given his last washing, drained of his blood, embalmed, his every pore closed, he filled the air with all these scents for me.

I longed to give him up now, since I must. To detach him from me and begin the process of transformation in my mind that his body must now undergo in the earth. I must relegate him to a life of mine now lost and irrecoverable, for only after I had done so would the wound of his death begin to scar over. I vowed to myself that night that I would not go to his funeral. This would pain my mother and would scandalize everybody else, but I was not going to go; nothing could make me.

I heard Old Red toll midnight out of the silence, and I thought how, after twelve, there is no thirteen on the clock; it starts over; and I thought how, at thirteen, my life was starting over.

In just a few hours I would be taken away. What my new life would be like I could only guess at, but I knew it would be totally different from the one that was ending, and that a totally different person from the one I had been would be needed to survive in it.

What kind of person had I been? Like an artist stepping back from his easel, an artist engaged in painting a self-portrait, I stood back from myself to assess the stage I had arrived at. I saw a friendly, open, trustful boy. One who was more self-confident than not, whose fears were small fears. One who was studious, ambitious, determined to succeed. Generally obedient, well behaved.

No more selfish than most only children. Working now
with the dash of an artist dissatisfied with his effort, I
wiped out this boy and made a fresh start, sketching in
one of altogether different make.

First of all, I was no longer a boy. Funeral services
for my boyhood would be held tomorrow. I was little—
nothing I could do about that; all the more necessity,
then, that I be cunning, sly, tough. Hurt beyond bearing,
and about to be transferred to a world ignorant of and
indifferent to my story, I must protect myself against all
further hurt. Without a father to run to for protection,
I must protect myself. Instead of open, I must be
guarded, instead of trustful, suspicious, instead of confi-
dent, afraid. Ambition? My task now was not to get
ahead but to get by.

Since few others would be concerned for me, I must
be self-concerned. I must save myself for myself. My
heart, if I ever got the pieces back together again, would
be like a mended plate: not for use. No more girls for
me. Inward: that was what I must become. Not outgoing
—inturning.

And skeptical of everything I was told.

The boy I had been had believed whatever he was
told on authority. Study, work, be good, and as surely
as the seasons succeeded one another, you would get
ahead, he was told. That boy, that trustful boy, that
tenderfoot (he was beginning to seem like that little
brother I had always wanted), what a little grind he had
been! Convicts never worked harder than he at his
homework. Good! Convicts trying to get their sentences
shortened had never minded their behavior more carefully than he. And where had his diligence and his good

conduct gotten him? Since studying and being good were hard and unpleasant and not to be relied on to pay off, the smart people, the ones who until now I had thought were the stupid ones, were those grasshoppers who lived for today, for themselves, who idled away their time, knowing it might be the last they would ever have, and that if it were not—if it were succeeded by more—it still had been well spent.

My father had known that. The lesson of his life was: live, don't learn. For tomorrow you die—if you last that long; today is not over yet. Then the living they can't take from you, and the learning you can't take with you.

Henceforth, in exile, I would go my lone way. Neither country nor communion for me. No more parades, no flags, no fireworks for me. Our national holiday, The Glorious Fourth, would commemorate my loss—a time for others to celebrate, for me to mourn. I was one of its highway statistics.

One event, scheduled for the coming Sunday, I would have cancelled now even if I had been staying on in Clarksville.

Although my father called himself a "pagan," and had never been inside a church in my lifetime, and although my mother was never more than a fitful church-goer, they had decided—or rather, she had decided, and he was indifferent—about a year earlier, that as I came to the age of discretion, and was thus accountable for my sins, the safe thing would be to have me confirmed. Her aim was not religious or moral enlightenment for me, but merely a cheap kind of afterlife insurance.

I went along with it rather than make trouble. But

ever since my drowning I had had doubts that there was a life after death. My doubts shocked my mother, and so I kept them to myself. But I was unable to put them down. After all, I had had an experience my mother had not had. I had brought back with me from death no memory of an afterlife.

My mother, the few times I had spoken to her on the subject, said the reason for that was that I was not really dead.

"Oh, yes, I was, Mother. I most certainly was. I didn't know a thing. I was really dead."

"No, you weren't. Nobody is brought back from death. When you're dead you're dead."

"Jesus raised Lazarus. The Bible says so."

"Well, you're not Lazarus—and, though I'm grateful for him, your Cousin Ramsay Floyd is certainly not Jesus Christ!"

So I quit arguing with her about it. Maybe I was not quite one hundred percent dead, but I was near enough to it that I ought to have had a glimpse of Heaven— say, like Clarksville seen from the City Limit sign.

I was to have been confirmed the Sunday my father got hurt. Because that was the Fourth of July, my confirmation had been postponed. Now I shrank from God as I did from my relatives. I disowned my heavenly father who had orphaned me of my earthly one. It never entered my mind that God might have punished my father for his sins and his lack of faith. My thoughts were totally self-centered. I thought He was being cruel to me—me, who had been such a good boy.

A country ballad, newish, reflecting the new age of speed, but with the timeless quality they all had, sang itself in my mind. It went:

I heard the crash on the highway.
I knew what it was from the start.
I went to the scene of destruction,
A picture was stamped on my heart.

The whiskey and blood ran together,
Mixed up with blood where they lay,
Death lay her hand in destruction,
But I didn't hear nobody pray.

I didn't hear nobody pray, either. I heard the crash on the highway, I rushed to the scene of destruction, the picture was stamped on my heart: it was my father's blood that lay thick on the highway, and I didn't hear nobody pray. Mere chance shaped life; there was no God. This disbelief, I knew, isolated me still further from everyone I knew.

My last night's sleep in Clarksville, with my father's body lying in the next room, would be my last ever, I vowed. No visits home for me, no reopening of wounds. It was a vow I was to keep for thirty-two years.

WHEN JAMES I, KING OF ENGLAND, was asked why he was going back, after a long absence, to visit his native Scotland, he replied, "The salmon instinct."

The salmon is in his early adolescence when he leaves his native stream, impelled by an irresistible urge for something he has never known, the salt, salt sea. There he stays for the rest of his life, until he feels another prompting equally irresistible, the urge to reproduce himself. This the salmon can do only in that same stream in which he was born. And so, from distances as great as fifteen hundred miles, the old salmon heads for home.

Many things can, and do, kill the salmon on his long voyage home, but nothing can deter or detour him. Not the diseases and parasites he is prone to, not fishermen, commercial or sporting, not the highest falls. He endures them, he eludes them, he leaps them, impelled by his ardent homesickness. Though long an expatriate, he knows his nationality as a naturalized American knows his, and back to the country of his birth he goes, as though throughout all the years away he has kept his first passport. Through the pathless sea he finds his way unerringly to the river down which he came on his voyage out long ago, and past each of its tributaries, each more temptingly like the one he is seeking the nearer he gets to that special one, as towns in the same county are similar but not the same. When he gets to his, he knows it—as I, for instance, know Clarksville, and would know it even if, like the salmon, I had but one sense to lead me to it. The name given the salmon in Latin is *Salmo salar*: the fish that will leap waterfalls to get back home. Some later Linnaeus of the human orders must have classed me at birth among the Humphreys: in Welsh the name means "One who loves his hearth and home."

But I began to doubt my homing instincts, to think I had wandered too far away, stayed gone too long, when, after crossing the ocean, I went back those thirty-two years later.

I had spent a few days in Dallas first, as the homecoming salmon spends a few days in the estuary to reaccustom himself to sweet water after all his years at sea before ascending to his native stream; for although that is what he now longs for, those uterine waters of his, too sudden a change from the salt is a shock to him. Dallas had always been brackish to me.

The nearer I got to Clarksville the farther from it I seemed to be. This was not where I was spawned. Strange places had usurped the names of towns I used to know. It was like what the British during World War II, fearing an invasion, had done, setting real but wrong place-names and roadsigns around the countryside so that the enemy in, say, Kent would find himself in villages belonging to Lancashire.

Gone were the spreading cottonfields I remembered, though this was the season when they should have been beginning to whiten. The few patches that remained were small and sparse, like the patches of snow lingering on in sunless spots in New England in March and April. The prairie grass that had been there before the fields were broken for cotton had reclaimed them. The woods were gone—even Sulphur Bottom, that wilderness into which my father had gone in pursuit of the fugitive gunman: grazing land now, nearly all of it. For in a move that reverses Texas history, a move totally opposite to what I knew in my childhood, one which all but turns the world upside down, which makes the sun set in the East, Red River County has ceased to be Old South and become Far West. I who for years had had to set my Northern friends straight by pointing out that I was a Southerner, not a Westerner, and that I had never seen a cowboy or for that matter a beefcow any more than they had, found myself now in that Texas of legend and the popular image which when I was a child had seemed more romantic to me than to a boy of New England precisely because it was closer to me than to him and yet still worlds away. Gone from the square were the bib overalls of my childhood when the farmers came to town on Saturday. Ranchers now, they came in high-heeled boots and rolled-brim hats, a costume that would have provoked as much surprise, and even more derision, there, in my time, as it would on Manhattan's Madison Avenue.

You can never ascend the same river twice, an early philosopher tells us. Its course, its composition are ever changing. Even so, one of its natives knows it, even one, like the salmon, who has spent most of his life away. I had been away from Clarksville since my father's death, and although ever since then I had been surprised each day to find myself alive, I was now an older man than he had lived to be. In that time much had changed in Clarksville; still, it was where I belonged.

Just as the salmon must leave home when the time comes, so he must return to round out his life. There where he was born, he dies.

Two boys, out of school, were playing in the Clarksville cemetery, where I had played as a boy, and seeing my guide and me wandering about looking for something we could not find, they came over and offered to lead us to any grave we might be seeking; they knew the cemetery well, they lived nearby and played there every day. Looking at either of them was like looking at myself through the wrong end of binoculars. I gave them half a dollar apiece, a token repayment for all the many nickels that men of Clarksville had given me in my time, and taking into account the devaluation of the currency since my time; thanked them; said no, we were not looking for any grave, what we were looking for was just the opposite: some spot where there was not any grave, where there was still room for one. Why? Was somebody dead? No; not yet.

So instead they helped us in this search, and, on the street side of the cemetery, not far from the Hanging Tree, we found one. I bought it on the spot—my last piece of real estate. Fitting, said my guide—an ex-mayor of the town, the one who had condemned and torn down the grammar school, my favorite uncle, my mother's youngest brother, the only one of the Varley tribe who had stayed in Clarksville, the rest now scattered to the four winds—very fitting.

"I mean, that it should be so near the house where you were born," he explained. "There's something fitting in that."

"That house was torn down shortly after I was born in it. I never even knew where it stood."

"Torn down? Who ever told you that?"

"I was always told that. My mother told me. I wondered about that house a lot. She told me it was torn down shortly after I was born."

"Well, it's still standing right where it's always stood. Still lived in."

"You're sure it's the same house?"

"I've known it all my life. I came to see you in it when you were one day old. You want to see it? It's, like I say, right near here."

I followed him to the back of the cemetery, down the path I used to take when Old Red warned me I might be late for school, to the lane I used to hurry through, embarrassed by and afraid of its inhabitants. The only change there since my time was that the junk cars in the yards were later models.

"It's that one there," said my uncle with a nod, and

I understood then why my mother, ashamed for me to see it, had razed that hovel from her memory, and from mine.

Old Red still tolled, though without the four, eight, twelve and sixteen chimes before the quarter, half, three-quarters and the hour that I remembered. It never had, said my uncle softly, loath to destroy an old and cherished, but erroneous impression of mine. When I heard it now, a momentary reddishness overspread my sight and I smelled the most appetizing of all aromas. Or rather, I imagined I did; the cotton gone, the cottonseed mill was gone, too. One of the many changes, losses. The Confederate soldier in the plaza had been twisted around on his column. He now faced northeast, as though just setting off for the war, but I remembered distinctly that he faced southwest, and looked as though he had just gotten back, on foot, all the way from Appomattox. The town had shrunk, fit closer, like old clothes long outgrown. So much smaller now than when measured by my ten-, eleven-, twelve-year-old stride, and when, as Old Red told me then, I had all the time in the world.